A Teacher's Guide to Curriculum Design for Gifted and Advanced Learners

A Teacher's Guide to Curriculum Design for Gifted and Advanced Learners provides educators with models and strategies they can easily use to create appropriately complex differentiated lessons, questions, tasks, and projects. This must-have resource for both gifted and regular education teachers:

- Includes specific thinking models for teaching English language arts, social studies, and STEM.
- Is ideal for teachers who are looking for ways to differentiate and design lessons for their highest achieving students.
- Provides multiple examples of how to embed complexity within standards-based lessons.
- Highlights units and models from Vanderbilt University's Programs for Talented Youth curriculum.
- Helps teachers provide the necessary challenge for advanced learners to thrive.

The models have been vetted by content experts in the relevant disciplines and were designed to guide students to develop expertise within a discipline. Definitions of widely used terms, such as *depth*, *complexity*, and *abstractness*, are explained and linked to models within specific content areas to support common understanding and application of schoolwide differentiation strategies.

Tamra Stambaugh, PhD, is an Associate Professor and Margo Long Endowed Chair in Gifted Education, Whitworth University, USA. She has over 25 years' experience in gifted education.

Emily Mofield, EdD, is an Assistant Professor in the College of Education at Lipscomb University, USA. She has over 20 years' experience teaching gifted students and leading gifted services.

A Teacher's Guide to Curriculum Design for Gifted and Advanced Learners

Advanced Content Models for Differentiating Curriculum

Tamra Stambaugh and Emily Mofield

NEW YORK AND LONDON

Cover image by Allegra Denbo

First published 2022
by Routledge
605 Third Avenue, New York, NY 10158

and by Routledge
2 Park Square, Milton Park, Abingdon, Oxon, OX14 4RN

Routledge is an imprint of the Taylor & Francis Group, an informa business

© 2022 Taylor & Francis

The right of Tamra Stambaugh and Emily Mofield to be identified as authors of this work has been asserted in accordance with sections 77 and 78 of the Copyright, Designs and Patents Act 1988.

All rights reserved. No part of this book may be reprinted or reproduced or utilised in any form or by any electronic, mechanical, or other means, now known or hereafter invented, including photocopying and recording, or in any information storage or retrieval system, without permission in writing from the publishers.

Trademark notice: Product or corporate names may be trademarks or registered trademarks, and are used only for identification and explanation without intent to infringe.

Library of Congress Cataloging-in-Publication Data
A catalog record for this title has been requested

ISBN: 978-1-032-14513-6 (hbk)
ISBN: 978-1-64632-223-7 (pbk)
ISBN: 978-1-003-23851-5 (ebk)

DOI: 10.4324/9781003238515

Typeset in Palatino
by Apex CoVantage, LLC

Contents

1 Talent Development and the Development of Expertise and Creative Production 1

2 Definitions and Models for Differentiation: An Introduction 4

3 Models for Differentiating Instruction in English Language Arts – Literature 20

4 Models for Differentiating Instruction Using English Language
   Arts – Informational Texts 34

5 Models for Differentiating Instruction in Social Studies 47

6 Models for Differentiating Instruction in the STEM Fields 68

7 Models for Incorporating Visual Analysis of Art 78

8 Creating Interdisciplinary and Intradisciplinary Connections 87

9 Making Differentiation Work: Additional Considerations 95

   Appendices 103
   Appendix A Models for Complexity: Blank/Annotated Wheels 103
   A1 Introduction to Using Analysis Wheels 104
   A2 Literary Analysis Wheel – Primary and Literary Analysis Wheel 106
   A3 Fictional Writing Wheel 112
   A4 Text Analysis Wheel – Primary 115
   A5 Rhetorical Analysis Wheel 119
   A6 Argumentative Writing Wheel 122
   A7 Social Studies Connections Wheel 126
   A8 Primary Source Analysis Wheel 129
   A9 STEM Analysis Wheel 132
   A10 Visual Analysis Wheel 136

   Appendix B Models for Depth 139
   B1 Choice-Reasoning Chart – Humanities 140
   B2 Problem-Reasoning Chart – STEM 142

   Appendix C Models for Abstractness 145
   C1 Concept Organizer 146
   C2 Big Idea Reflection 148

   References 150
   Authors' Biographies 153

Talent Development and the Development of Expertise and Creative Production

An aim of this book is to provide models for designing learning experiences that support students on a trajectory of developing expertise. Eventually, when students leave our classrooms and enter their fields of study, we want them to be skilled in applying their knowledge and creativity in solving real-world problems as experts do. What does it mean to think and practice as an expert? How do we support students on this trajectory when they are learning the building blocks of a discipline at a young age? What do we know about the development of expertise and how does this fit within the context of gifted education? This chapter addresses these questions.

Development of Expertise

A number of factors influence the development of expertise including motivation, support from mentors, and access to rigorous curriculum that emphasizes methodologies of a discipline (Subotnik et al., 2011). In the chapters that follow, we describe how curriculum can be designed to support the development of expertise, but first we must consider, what does it mean to think as an expert? Bransford et al. (2000) and Adams et al. (2008) provide the following insight on expert-like thinking:

- Experts have developed a sophisticated mental framework for organizing knowledge. They understand nuances and relationships within and among various ideas and systems and understand the interrelatedness of ideas.
- Experts solve problems and ask important questions. They spend a considerable amount of time defining and understanding a problem.
- Experts understand big ideas and assimilate knowledge into key ideas, themes, generalizations, theories, or laws. They understand patterns among concepts and use these patterns to make decisions and know next steps.
- Experts reflect on their learning and know when to revise ideas.
- Experts have the psychosocial skills necessary to achieve.

DOI: 10.4324/9781003238515-1

TABLE 1.1 Curriculum considerations for developing expertise

Curriculum Area	Questions to Consider for Developing Expertise
Content	• What expertise does the content address? • Who would typically study this content? (historian, writer, analyst, etc.) • Who already knows the content? What content is necessary to teach so that students can access the next level of understanding and expertise?
Process	• How would a _____ think about this? • What processes, tools, or resources would a _____ use? How? • What would an expert do in this situation?
Product	• What types of products might an expert create? • What criteria would be valid for measuring the importance of the product?
Concept/Law/Generalizations	• What rules, or theories are necessary to understand this? How do these transfer into patterns, generalizations, or key understandings that I can clearly state or readily apply? In what situations might these key understandings need to be modified? • How can I organize what I know into two or three key ideas that would be true in multiple situations? • What patterns have I surmised about my content and processes that are true or applied in most situations? (Generalizations)
Habits of the Discipline	• How would an expert communicate this appropriately? • What access or opportunities would be appropriate to take or provide here? • Does everyone have similar access? If not, how can I provide it? • What affective skills would an expert need in this situation? How can I teach these skills? (goal setting, effective communication, understanding one's strengths and limitations, perseverance, risk taking, working in a group)

Source: Adapted from Stambaugh (2018), p. 111, Table 5.3. Prufrock Press. Used with permission.

If we understand what experts do and how they think, we can intentionally plan curriculum and learning experiences to prepare students to engage with content as experts do within their respective fields. Table 1.1 provides examples and questions to ask as part of curriculum planning. As noted in the table, you will see guiding questions for curriculum development to consider what experts know, how they think about content, how they produce new knowledge, and how they organize their knowledge around principles and ideas that generalize to multiple situations. Additionally, you can consider how to support students' trajectories toward expertise through cultivating their habits of achievement, including access to opportunities and the development of psychosocial skills.

Talent Development

The talent development model in gifted education focuses on cultivating students' strengths and talents within a specific domain in order to transform potential to ability, ability into competence, and competence into expertise (Subotnik et al., 2011). This model is based on the assumption that abilities are malleable and can be nurtured in supportive contexts. This cultivation of talent happens on a continuum in different stages and at different trajectories, depending on a student's readiness level, access to opportunities, and the specific discipline. Several factors are necessary for talent development including motivation, access and exposure to high level content, and cultivation of psychosocial skills (e.g., mental skills needed to achieve set goals and counter setbacks).

We must emphasize that it is critically important for students to have access to high-quality curriculum. In many ways, it is the key to unlocking future opportunities in students' lives. When students interact with curriculum designed to support the development of expertise, they not only develop habits of thinking in the discipline but also have opportunities to develop positive habits of achievement, including self-agency, perseverance, and self-regulation skills. Curriculum serves as an equalizer for opportunity because it promotes access to rich learning experiences that open doors to next steps in talent development.

The chapters that follow focus on designing or adapting curriculum so that students can move toward their next steps on their talent trajectories, specifically with exposure to reading, writing, and thinking as experts do. These models make the invisible patterns of expert-like thinking visible by making the connections between concepts explicit. When these structures and connections are continually applied and practiced in various contexts, students begin to perceive and internalize the underlying principles of the discipline.

If students have opportunities to interact with content as experts do, they can apply their learning in creative ways. This includes developing authentic products, evaluating multiple perspectives, making insightful connections, modeling phenomena, asking new questions, and elaborating upon ideas. For example, when students understand the structure of a discipline, they can understand how the structure can be modified or improved. This comes into play in lessons where students develop solution ideas or consider multiple points of view. Also, as students understand more about the connections between concepts within a content area, they can make insightful connections as they uncover nuances within these relationships. You will find these models provide many opportunities for students to ask new questions, create models, apply what they are learning in innovative ways given specific criteria, and generate multiple ideas, solutions, and connections – all important processes related to how experts engage in the creative process.

The models and tools in this resource build mental structures that become stronger and more sophisticated as students examine the interconnected relationships across concepts and ideas. These models also allow students to grapple with real-world issues through exploring multiple perspectives and applying overarching generalizations (big ideas) within and across disciplines. Overall, these models enhance the development of expertise and creative production by building a strong, organized structure of knowledge as a foundation for examining patterns among concepts and determining next steps in solving problems.

So, how do we actually teach students to think this way? Our aim is to simplify the complexity. We hope you find the models that follow to be simple tools for supporting students' complex thinking!

2

Definitions and Models for Differentiation: An Introduction

How we define differentiation, particularly for academically advanced learners, is important. We cannot apply differentiation strategies if we do not know what it means to differentiate, what works in developing talent, or how experts think about topics within their respective disciplines. In this chapter we outline our operational definitions of acceleration, depth, complexity, abstractness, and creativity that are used throughout this book and also provide some general principles and ideas for differentiating instruction using the discussed definitions and subsequent models associated with each definition. Throughout this book we model how accelerated materials, depth, complexity, and abstractness can be used to differentiate instruction and promote higher-level thinking in each content discipline.

Before we discuss specific content-based models for each definition, let's first look at an overall model for curriculum development, differentiation, and the development of expertise. This model (see Figure 2.1) is a synthesis of the expertise and talent development literature discussed in Chapter 1 with the Integrated Curriculum Model (ICM) (VanTassel-Baska, 1986), an evidence supported curriculum design model that has been well researched with complementary curriculum resources provided for gifted and academically advanced students. The ICM has been in existence for over 35 years and has a solid and longstanding history of garnering positive and important academic achievement gains in a variety of content domains when applied with fidelity. (Also see VanTassel-Baska & Stambaugh, 2007 for earlier discussions about these combined models and the effectiveness of the ICM curriculum over time.) You will notice in Figure 2.1 that curriculum development and differentiation for academically advanced learners involves a combination of three key components: accelerated resources/content/standards; discipline-specific models and processes; and connections to concepts, theories, and laws. *The more components that are integrated together, the more rigorous and differentiated the task demands will be.* For example, incorporating the next grade-level standards (acceleration) for students who are ready to move to the next level is not as rigorous as applying the next grade-level's standards (acceleration) *with* higher level questions that are common in the discipline (processes of experts such as depth and complexity). Then you could add another layer and link the content and processes to big ideas in the field such as theories, laws, or universal themes or ask students to create new generalizations based on their current learning (abstractness).

As noted in the model, acceleration involves content and pacing. The processes and products of experts embed depth, complexity, and product design as part of creative synthesis, and the conceptual component of the model involves connecting and synthesizing ideas across disciplines. Each of these strategies can be used as a single-faceted way to differentiate or these can be combined to add even more advanced instruction for students who are ready for the next level of challenge

DOI: 10.4324/9781003238515-2

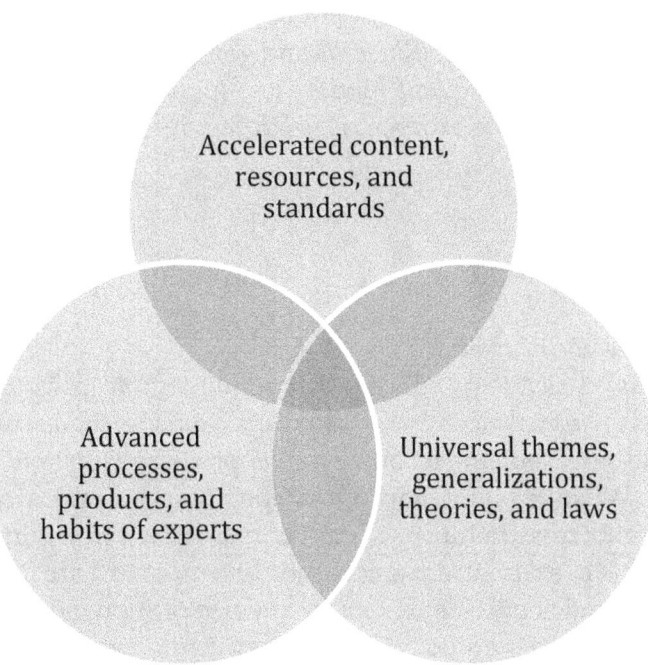

FIGURE 2.1 Differentiated Curriculum Design Model
Source: Adapted from VanTassel-Baska (1986) p. 165.

TABLE 2.1 Definitions of differentiation with support models and strategies

Habits of Expert	Curriculum Response and Differentiation Feature/Definition	Supporting Models and Strategies
Experts more quickly assimilate and process information learned	**Accelerate** the content 1. Provide students with more advanced content AND 2. Adjust the pacing and instructional level of content standards and materials/resources	• Subject Acceleration • Curriculum Compacting • Academically Advanced Resources for the Grade Level
Experts solve real-world problems and examine problems and solutions through multiple lenses, perspectives, and scenarios	Add **depth** 1. Add a debatable question or problem-based scenario AND 2. Examine it through multiple resources, problems	• Choice-Reasoning Chart in Humanities • Problem-Reasoning Chart – STEM (Appendix B)
Experts understand and account for the interactions and relationships among multiple variables	Make tasks and questions more **complex** 1. Add content-specific variables or elements AND 2. Examine the relationships among the said variables	• Content-Based Analysis Wheels (Appendix A)
Experts assimilate or chunk information into usable categories and key ideas	Link facts and new learning to **abstract** ideas 1. Add a concept, theory, or law AND 2. Create new generalizations or link newly learned information to predetermined generalizations, theories, or laws	• Concept Maps • Big Idea Reflection (Appendix C)
Experts create original and relevant products/solutions to further the knowledge in their field.	Require authentic products with **specific criteria** 1. Ask students to create authentic products AND 2. Add specific criteria that include depth, complexity, and/or abstractness	• Criteria-based templates • "That" and "and" stems

(i.e., accelerating a reading text but asking simple questions versus accelerating a reading text and asking more complex questions that link to concepts and generalizations). Next, we explain and define each differentiation strategy and subsequent models to support each strategy. An overview of definitions and models including how the models relate to the development of expertise is outlined in Table 2.1 and will serve as an outline for this chapter.

Differentiation Feature: Acceleration

Adjust the pacing and level of content/resources.

Accelerate first and then enrich (e.g., add depth, complexity, or abstractness). As we think about the definitions and models set forth in this book, we are making the assumption that the content, grade-level standards, reading levels, and resources are appropriately matched to the student's level of readiness and experience. When applying appropriate depth and complexity strategies, as explained in the next section, acceleration may naturally occur because the act of solving real-world problems or combining multiple elements to examine a phenomenon, event, or text are likely to include knowledge from the next set of grade-level standards or require the use of more advanced texts, resources, and concepts. Of course, we must keep the student's level of maturity, readiness, experience, and interests in mind as well when planning for accelerated opportunities. For more information about the types of acceleration and the impact of specific types on student learning, you can also check out the resources from the Acceleration Institute (www.accelerationinstitute.org).

While there are many forms of acceleration, we emphasize two discipline-specific ways to accelerate within a grade level: 1) subject acceleration or the use of above-grade level resources and content standards matched to documented student readiness and performance, and 2) curriculum compacting or pre-assessing students to determine prior knowledge and then excusing them from known work so that they can focus on more advanced, in-depth, or complex activities instead of continuing with lessons or content they have already mastered. All differentiation strategies assume that student readiness, interest, and performance have been considered before students are matched to appropriate content.

Processes of Experts: Depth and Complexity

Depth and complexity are hallmarks of expert thinking. Experts identify and solve problems and understand the multiple layers involved in considering scenarios and solutions. We can support students to think in in-depth and complex ways by providing debatable questions in a field and by helping them understand that when they are analyzing texts, events, or phenomena that there are several factors that need to be considered simultaneously. We can therefore differentiate instruction and add more depth by incorporating real-world debatable questions or problems in a field and examining these ideas through multiple perspectives, resources, and ideas. This is our definition of depth: add a debatable question and examine it through multiple avenues.

Complexity, then, is defined as adding a variable or element and examining the relationship. The relationships and variables differ by content area. Models to support teacher differentiation and to organize student thinking have been created and are explained next.

Differentiation Feature: Depth
Add a debatable or forced-choice question, problem, problem-based scenario, or idea and examine it from multiple perspectives, processes, or resources.

Depth of thinking is best done when asking debatable or researchable questions that require students to evaluate scenarios, problems/solutions, or ideas from a variety of sources or perspectives. Depth questions support relevance in the curriculum and allow students to examine real-world issues within a discipline. These overarching questions or problem-based scenarios can be used to frame a unit or guide a discipline specific lesson. Questions or scenarios can be designed for individual lessons or to guide a unit. Depth questions are not intended to be judgment-based queries that lack textual or other evidential support nor are they to be ethically bound questions. Depth questions should be based on evidence that meets a standard, purpose, or goal and also considers the context of the district. Some debatable questions taken out of context could quickly become divisive or offensive. Table 2.2 provides examples within a unit of study that promote evaluation and synthesis.

Questions or scenarios can also be derived from topics or standards to guide a unit of study. Students could examine specific texts, models, experiments, or ideas to answer the question or to explore an issue. Table 2.3 provides examples of common standards and questions that promote evaluative and in-depth thinking. After the initial question is posed at the start of a unit, students read texts or conduct experiments as part of the typical unit of study planned. Then a layer of depth is added as students revisit the overarching depth question after new information is learned. Finally, students synthesize new information and justify their thinking about the question using facts gleaned throughout the course of the unit.

When creating depth questions, it is helpful to consider the following:

- ◆ Are there multiple perspectives, resources, or findings available on the topic?
- ◆ What problems or questions would an expert in the field ask?
- ◆ Is this question developmentally and contextually appropriate?
- ◆ Does the question allow for evaluation and synthesis of multiple sources or experiments?
- ◆ Does the question incorporate multiple grade level standards?

TABLE 2.2 Examples of topics and issues as depth questions

Topic	Issue or Debatable Question
Stamp Act	Can progress happen without conflict?
Bugs/ecology	Which bug is most important to the ecosystem and why? Should you kill spiders in your house?
Art or photograph analysis	Is this piece expressing more positive or negative feelings?
Fractions	Are fractions ratios? Are ratios fractions?
Book character	Is the character a rebel or a hero?

TABLE 2.3 Adding depth questions to standards

StandardStudents will be able to explain how....	Depth Question or Real-World and Applied Scenario
changes on Earth's surface over time is a result of natural processes and human activity.	Should we stop natural erosion?
living things depend upon each other and the environment to survive; have adaptations that help them survive; are impacted by physical conditions of the environment; use science to solve everyday problems.	Should we use pesticides to kill mosquitoes that spread disease?
there are multiple events that led to wars and its aftermath.	Does war bring unity or division?
one can interpret statistical reports in the media and other places by linking claims to data.	Are statistical reports facts?
the different characters and settings impact the conflict.	Do our experiences shape us or do we shape our experiences?

We need to help students keep track of multiple sources, experiments, or facts so they can appropriately evaluate and synthesize multiple sources. When students are learning how to reason in depth, models and frameworks can support their new learning. Appendix B provides two models for organizing the data, resources, processes, events, texts, or persons/characters of study around a debatable question. While we discuss debatable questions here, know that problem-based scenarios can be used instead of specific questions to add depth. Each of the discipline-specific chapters that follow in this book also provide detailed examples of how debatable questions or scenarios/problems are used to support in-depth thinking.

Differentiation Feature: Complexity
Add a variable and examine the relationships or connections.

Experts understand that when solving problems or analyzing and interpreting events, multiple relationships must be considered. In order to differentiate instruction and help students think in more complex ways we, as educators, need to help students understand the foundational elements that make up a field or thinking process and teach students how these elements or factors are interrelated. For example, historians who are interpreting a past event don't just consider the geographic location of the event, they also consider how geography, political influences, and economics impacted or influenced actions. Similarly, literary analysts understand that it is not simply one element that determines a theme. Instead, they examine how multiple elements influence the others. For example, setting influences characters and their motivation, which collectively leads to how one interprets the text or arrives at a theme. When planning for innovation, scientists don't just look at their own experiments and methods, they understand how cumulative scientific information can be replicated or built upon in ways that new methods or measures can be used to ask or model new questions, determine new patterns, or adjust the scale. As such, adding complexity as a differentiation strategy occurs by layering elements in ways that help students see connections and relationships between and among different variables.

Appendix A provides several content-specific models (or analysis wheels) to guide teachers in differentiating questions and activities and support students in thinking like an expert. The wheels were designed after studying content-based standards and talking with experts about how they think about texts, problems, or events in their field. As the wheels were designed, we shared the models again with experts in the field for vetting.

The analysis wheels support differentiated and complex instruction for the teacher and the learner. For example, teachers may use the wheels to differentiate tasks and questions or to model thinking by explicitly teaching the model to students or asking them to refer to the model when processing information. When modeling thinking, a gradual release approach that moves students from teacher-led modeling in a whole group setting to small group work and individual completion with follow-up discussions allows students the opportunity to make their own connections and work toward independence. The first time a student is exposed to the wheel, it is recommended that teachers explicitly model how to use the wheel, guiding students from simple to complex thinking questions – encouraging students to use the model as a way of thinking and asking questions every time they encounter a text, problem, event, experiment, or scenario. The goal is for students to internalize the thinking processes required in each discipline. After students are comfortable with the wheel, they may complete it on their own or in small groups, drawing arrows to show connections between different variables. Students may complete the wheel on their own as a prerequisite for a group discussion, Socratic seminar, debate, or experiment, for example.

The wheels can also be used as part of a tiered assignment as differentiated questions or tasks from the wheel can be assigned to various groups of students based on readiness and mastery of standards through learning centers, contracts, reading groups, or individualized instruction. Each content-specific chapter in this book provides more detailed examples for using the wheel

TABLE 2.4 Simple to complex differentiated question examples

Content Area	Simple Questions (single areas on the wheel)	Complex/Differentiated Questions (relationships or combination of at least two areas on the wheel)
ELA – Literary Analysis	What was the conflict in the story?	How did the interaction among the characters and the setting create the conflict?
Social Studies (Timelines)	Create a timeline of events that led to the fall of the Roman Empire.	Create a timeline of events that shows how at least two different factors on the Social Studies Connections Wheel interacted in a way that contributed to the fall of the Roman Empire.
STEM (Science, Technology, Engineering, and Math)	Draw a model that shows the water cycle steps.	Draw a model that shows how heat affects evaporation and condensation in the water cycle.

to differentiate questions. Similarly, several examples of completed wheels with arrows that show connections are provided in the subsequent content-based chapters. Appendix A also provides general question stems for asking simple and complex questions using each wheel. A few examples are also included in Table 2.4.

Instructional Management and Complexity

There are some instructional management considerations that we need to mention when using the wheels to differentiate instruction by adding complexity. First, the wheels are designed for use in teaching thinking processes. The wheels are not intended to be used as a worksheet or in ways that do not allow students opportunities to discuss ideas; teachers need to hear what students are thinking, the connections students are making, and provide feedback on student thinking so that students can continue to increase their level of understanding of complex relationships. Discussion with an emphasis on the complex relationships among different elements is an integral part of implementation. This final discussion needs to be guided by someone who is knowledgeable about the content so that misconceptions are questioned as students continue to examine complex relationships among the various elements listed in each wheel.

Second, the goal of the wheel is for students to examine complex relationships. Therefore, if students are completing the wheel, make sure they are creating arrows that show relationships among different parts of the wheel; be ready to ask them about the rationale for their arrows and relationships among the different elements or variables. If you are using the wheel to differentiate questions, make sure you are combining at least two sections on the wheel into a complex question. Use your content-based standards and outcomes to help you determine which areas of the wheel require the most emphasis. Finally, the wheel should not be used every day or even every week. The number of times you use a wheel is dependent upon the content and content area. If reading a novel in English Language Arts (ELA) perhaps the wheel would be completed twice throughout the reading of the novel. If you are outlining science phenomena or studying an event in social studies, perhaps the wheel is used once every couple of weeks as new information is learned or introduced.

Depending on student readiness, adding complexity to tasks or questions may not be enough of a challenge. Many of the current standards (especially in the upper grade ELA standards) already incorporate complexity with criteria for students to determine how elements contribute to other elements. Teachers may consider adding additional differentiation features such as depth and/or abstractness to tasks, assignments, or products as explained in this chapter. The layering of multiple differentiation features coupled with accelerated content, standards, and resources helps make tasks even more rigorous.

Differentiation Feature: Abstractness

Add a concept, theory, generalization or law and connect it to facts and ideas.

If you want to add abstractness to your lessons, help students connect concepts, generalizations, theories, or laws to facts and information previously learned. Students may also create their own generalizations by combining multiple concepts into a generalized statement. Why should we connect concepts and abstractness as part of a differentiated strategy? Learning transfers at the conceptual level (Erickson, 2008) and connections to generalizations and concepts encourages students to focus on the big ideas associated with facts and information. Linking concepts and generalizations to newly learned facts or creating common generalizations from facts supports students in making meaning and connections among multiple data points. It allows a frame for assimilating and organizing new information more quickly (Bransford et al, 2000).

So, what is the difference between a concept and a generalization? According to Taba (1962) a concept is a one-word idea (i.e., structure, freedom, systems, change, time), whereas a generalization is a more advanced statement that links multiple concepts together (i.e., change happens over time) and requires more critical thinking. Concepts and generalizations can be universal and interdisciplinary or discipline-specific. For example, concepts such as freedom or gravity are more likely to be limited to social studies and science, respectively, whereas macro or universal concepts such as structure, patterns, or systems have relevance in multiple subject areas. For example, the universal concept of structure can be applied across multiple disciplines. In music or art, students can discuss the structure of a piece; in math, students can discuss the structure of a problem; in social studies, students can discuss the structure of a government, and in ELA, students might discuss the structure of a poem or story. There are common lists of universal themes and generalizations readily available online. A simple web search of "universal themes and generalizations" will provide users with a handout of 10–12 common universal themes and subsequent generalizations such as change, systems, order and chaos, patterns, power, structure, etc. Some examples of concepts and generalizations are provided in Table 2.5.

TABLE 2.5 Examples of concepts with generalizations

Concept	*Generalizations*
Change	Change is linked to time. Change can be positive or negative. Change promotes change.
Power	Power can take on many forms. Power can be used or abused. Power is connected to a source.
Systems	Systems are made up of smaller systems that are interdependent. Systems have inputs, outputs, elements, and boundaries. When one part of a system changes the other parts of the system adapt.
Patterns	Patterns have segments that repeat. Patterns allow for prediction. Patterns have an internal order.

Source: Adapted from the *Curriculum Guide for the Education of Gifted High School Students*, Texas Association for the Gifted and Talented (1991).

TABLE 2.6 Examples of abstract differentiated tasks and questions

Subject Area	On Grade-Level Task (No Concepts/Generalizations Included)	*Differentiated Task with Abstractness* (Concepts/ Generalizations Added)
Math	Add and subtract 2-digit numbers	What patterns do you notice when adding and subtracting 2-digit numbers? Write a rule based on one of the patterns you notice. Explain how the pattern allows for prediction even if you don't know the specific answer.
ELA	Read the "Three Little Pigs" and summarize the key events of the story.	Read the "Three Little Pigs" and summarize the most important three changes that occurred throughout the course of the story.
Science	Illustrate the life cycle of a plant. Write a sentence that explains the key components of the life cycle.	Illustrate the life cycle of a plant and include and label at least two different inter-related systems that impact the plant's growth or lack thereof. Write a sentence that explains what would happen to different elements of the life cycle if one part of a system no longer functioned effectively.
Social Studies	Create a timeline of the key events that led to the Revolutionary War.	Create a timeline of events that led to a change in power in the Revolutionary War. Label the sources of power for each.

Table 2.6 shows ways to differentiate activities by adding a concept and a generalization. Subsequent chapters in this book also show examples for adding abstractness within particular disciplines. Note that a concept and generalization, not just a concept, are used to differentiate a task.

Models and Strategies for Adding Abstractness

In addition to using concepts and generalizations to differentiate questions and tasks, we highlight three specific models/strategies for adding abstractness to lessons:

1. Justify generalizations using concept maps and organizers so that students are able to connect newly learned information or facts to universal generalizations or content-specific generalizations, theories, or laws that govern that discipline (see Appendix C1).
2. Create one's own generalizations after discussing word banks of concepts and ideas.
3. Connect concepts to real-world scenarios using the Big Idea Reflection Guide (see Appendix C2).

Concept Maps and Concept Organizers

Students individually create or add to a class concept map using examples from content areas. The concept map typically has the concept in the middle and generalizations as "spokes." A concept map might also include specific lesson topics or texts that students connect to the concept(s). Instead of adding concept generalizations as part of concept map outshoots, the spokes could be a story, experiment, article, or other prompt. If using this concept map strategy, it is important to emphasize that students use specific generalizations as part of their description if these are not explicit. Alternately, especially in STEM fields, content-specific units could list a theory or law in the center (i.e., Newton's Laws) with the specific principles (i.e., an object at rest remains at rest . . .) as offshoots for students to link facts and ideas from experiments or texts.

Concept map working walls (basically creating a wall-sized concept map that students can manipulate or add to by using sticky notes and tape or string to make connections among multiple generalizations and newly learned facts) can be developed over time as students read additional texts or draw upon information from other disciplines. Some teachers have found it helpful to use different colored paper or markers to signify disciplines or lessons. For example, connections to a concept in science may be in green, while social studies connections may be in red. Students can use painter's tape to link ideas and facts together and branch out from specific generalizations. Different colored paper can be used for different student groups or subject areas. The students add facts, statements, or examples to support the generalizations.

Figure 2.2 shows how the concept and generalizations for structure might begin as part of a working wall or handout. Students would add to each generalization as applicable, citing specific examples, facts, or inferences from their text, source, or discipline. Students may also draw connecting arrows or use linking words and string to connect different concepts and generalizations to others. For example, after reading a poem students may place a statement such as "the alliterated and choppy AB rhyming pattern helped the reader understand the struggle of the character" beside the generalization on the wall that says, "parts of a structure interact to achieve a purpose."

Concept walls and maps can be used as learning centers and also as a way to check for understanding. Some teachers have used working walls as assessments, checks for understanding, and exit tickets. In this way students add a sticky note with justification of newly learned information to the appropriate generalization on the wall and teachers use student responses to differentiate the next set of lessons, correct misconceptions, reteach, or even grade responses. If there isn't enough space in the classroom for a working wall or you prefer that students connect their facts to generalizations on their own to multiple sources, Appendix C1: Concept Organizer provides an alternative to the concept map. The Concept Organizer may be kept in a journal and completed as new sources are added to a unit of study. Using this organizer, students are able to compare generalizations and concepts from multiple sources on one page.

Regardless of the concept map used, it is also important that students understand that multiple concepts are possible and that multiple concepts besides the one selected for a specific lesson or unit may be applicable. Therefore, explicitly requesting that students show connections to other concepts (e.g., structure and progress, not just structure) encourages them to think about other abstract applications and relationships.

Adding Abstractness by Writing Generalizations

Another approach for incorporating abstractness is to provide a list of concept words or word banks that relate to the content being studied. For example, if examining a piece of art such as *A Sunday Afternoon on the Island of La Grande Jatte*, the word list might be *togetherness, relaxation, peace, recreation, community, interactions, nature, beauty, warmth*, etc. This concept list serves as a word bank from which students create a sentence using at least two of these words that capture a major idea from the art. Students may write "Interacting with nature and with others brings relaxation" to convey an idea that generalizes beyond the art. If studying gravity in astronomy students may select from a word bank of concepts such as *gravity, force, orbit, mass,* and *acceleration*. Students could use the word bank to write a generalization about gravity such as "The lower the mass of an object the greater the pull of gravity." If students are studying addition and subtraction, concepts might be *patterns, increase, decrease, even, odd,* and *sum*. You could ask students to write as many true statements as possible using these words and then provide a problem that supports their statement. These concept words or word banks are a great way to help students connect multiple concepts together and begin to connect their own learning to create more abstract ideas, rules, generalizations, theories, or laws.

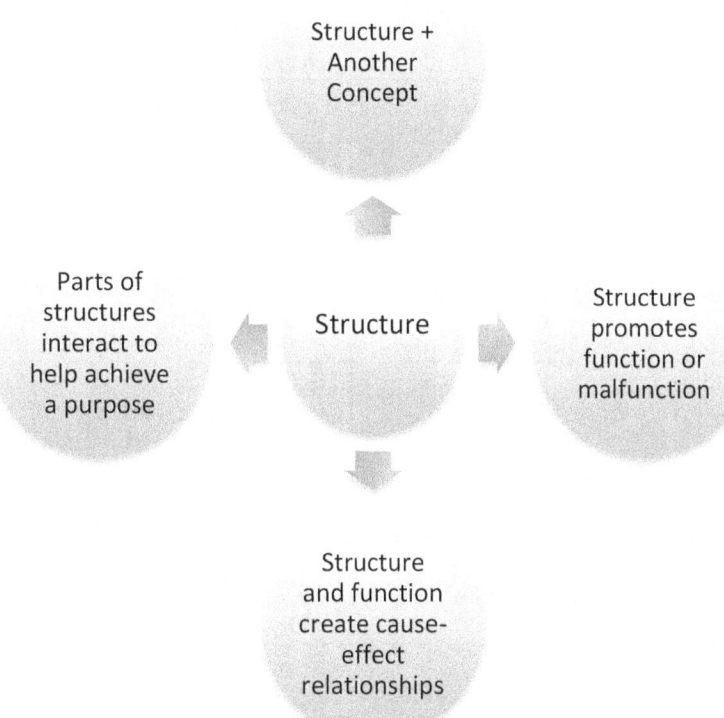

FIGURE 2.2 Concept map with generalizations

Abstractness and the Big Idea Reflection

The Big Idea Reflection is another way for students to think about concepts. Specifically, students can think about how those concepts relate to each other and how those concepts apply to students' lives. This framework allows the students to consider the major ideas within the content area and then consider how these concepts relate to broad generalizations, issues in the current world, and students themselves. The Big Idea Reflection helps students recognize these ideas about life in a way that integrates the content with the learner.

Figure 2.3 shows an example of how concepts can be connected using the Big Idea Reflection with example student responses as applied to the art piece, *Starry Night* by Van Gogh. This reflection can be used in any subject area to connect concepts to the real world. Though it is best used in the humanities, the Big Idea Reflection can also be used in STEM fields to connect experiments or ideas to real-world problems and scenarios.

Applying Depth, Complexity, and Abstractness to Differentiate Standards

Standards are an important part of a statewide accountability system and consequently a school-based emphasis. A focus on the standards as a basis or benchmark can serve as a guide for differentiating instruction while ensuring that students have appropriately mastered the standards necessary for a given grade level. While acceleration is a highly effective strategy there are ways that a grade-level standard or activity can be differentiated without moving directly to the next grade-level standard.

Big Idea Reflection – Example: *Starry Night* – Vincent Van Gogh		
		Sample Student Responses
What	**Concepts** What concepts/ideas are depicted?	Peace, despair, hope, calmness, movement, confusion, perception, duality of emotion
	Generalizations What broad statement can you make about one or more of these concepts? Make it generalizable beyond the text.	Art can convey a duality of emotion. Calmness can coexist with confusion.
So What	**Issue** What is the main issue, problem, or conflict?	The sky is brighter than the city at night – which is not a typical representation of such a scene. The techniques convey a swirling of sky, perhaps a swirling rush of emotion.
	Insight on Life What insight on life is provided by this text?	The art does not reflect a "real" reflection of reality –it shows an exaggerated view of the heavens. He challenges us to see beyond the normal "real" sky to perceive its exaggerated brightness. There is "light" within the dark.
Now What?	**World-Community-Individual** How does this text relate to you, your community, or your world? What question does the author want you to ask yourself?	This allows me to think about the duality of light and dark, hope and despair, chaos and calm. These ideas exist together, creating a sense of movement in emotion and thought.
	Implications How should you respond to the ideas in the text? What action should you take? What are the implications of the text? What can you do with this information?	This art makes me self-aware of my own duality of emotions. This art makes me interested in learning more about Van Gogh's life and any symbolism associated with the stars.

FIGURE 2.3 Big Idea Reflection example – Starry Night

To differentiate using standards, apply the aforementioned features of depth, complexity, or abstractness to the standard and then design a new activity that focuses on the more in-depth, complex, or abstract standard. Depending on student readiness, it is possible that many students could handle a differentiated standard at the onset of instruction with scaffolding as opposed to asking them to master a standard first and then to differentiate it. Table 2.7 shows examples of differentiated standards for adding depth, complexity, and abstractness.

Applying Depth, Complexity, and Abstractness to Products

When we teach in a way that incorporates depth, complexity, and abstractness, the products or tasks we require must reflect the advanced thinking as well. Product creation serves multiple purposes: 1) products provide an opportunity for students to practice synthesizing and applying new knowledge in creative ways; 2) student-created products allow educators to visibly see what students are thinking so that we can check for understanding and correct misconceptions; 3) products allow us, as educators, to see what students are able to create independently, so that we can determine their level of performance; and 4) products provide a way for students to practice the habits of an expert and create products similar to those of practicing professionals.

So, what do we need to know about products and product creation as part of developing expertise and creative production? Add criteria. Experts are bound by specific criteria or constraints. Whether experts are conducting an experiment, designing a structure, submitting an article for publication,

TABLE 2.7 Examples for differentiating standards

Standard	Differentiated Standard	Grade-Level Task Based on the Standard	Differentiated Task Based on New Standard	How Differentiated
(Florida: SS.K.C.2.3- Grade Kindergarten) Describe fair ways for groups to make decisions.	Describe fair ways for groups to make decisions by justifying opinions regarding majority rules.	Make a list of ways groups can make decisions. Which one do you think is the fairest and why?	Should the majority make decisions for the group? Defend your answer and compare it to other ways groups make decisions.	Depth is added by incorporating a debatable question and a required stance on the fairness of the majority and multiple perspectives or comparisons.
(ELA-LITERACY.RI.5.2) Determine two or more main ideas of a text and explain how they are supported by key details.	Determine how the author uses emotion and logic to support the claim of the text.	Write a paragraph to explain two different main ideas in the text and provide an example from the text that supports each main idea.	Write a paragraph that explains how the author uses the interaction of emotion and logic to support the claim.	Complexity is added by incorporating interactions among elements in the text and synthesizing main ideas to support a claim.
(NGSS 3-ESS3-1) Make a claim about the merit of a design solution that reduces the impacts of a weather-related hazard.	Analyze the relationship between the design and its effect on reducing flooding. Make recommendations for adjustments.	Given a solution, explain whether or not the solution will work to reduce flooding.	Given a solution for reducing flooding, make a recommendation for improving the solution, pointing out the weakest design points. Explain a) which parts of the structure were changed and why; and b) why the structure of your design is better.	Complexity is added by incorporating the relationship between the design structure and the intended effect. Abstractness is also added as students are examining how parts of the structure work together to achieve a purpose and that the structure is only as strong as its weakest part.
(CCSS Math NT 5 NBT.B.5) Fluently multiply multi-digit whole numbers using the standard algorithm.	Fluently multiply multi-digit whole numbers, identifying patterns and predicting possible solutions.	Multiply a set of ten 2- and 3-digit numbers (e.g., 27 x 54; 426 x 70; etc.). Show your work and be ready to explain your process for problem solving.	Solve for the following set of ten problems (e.g., 426 x 70; 27 x 54). Identify a pattern and write a rule for multiplying numbers. (Ideas: what happens when a number ends in 0? Are there differences in the process for multiplying in 2 versus 3-digit numbers; are there patterns when multiplying odd and even versus odd and odd numbers? etc.)	Abstractness is added as students are asked to determine and justify patterns and create a rule or generalization based on the pattern.

creating a presentation, or solving a problem there are specific criteria that they must follow. Creative productivity occurs within boundaries. Experts follow certain rules within their field. Therefore, adding criteria for student projects authenticates the experience and also guides teacher feedback and evaluation. The inclusion of criteria also promotes advanced thinking as students are required to work within confines of content and apply specific ideas in ways that may not have been considered previously. Criteria promote depth and complexity over breadth. For example, instead of asking students to write a new ending to a story, we can add criteria by asking students to create a new ending to a story that shows the interactions among the characters and setting. In this way, the task is still open-ended but forces students to think in more complex ways about the relationship between different factors.

Sentence stems that use two simple words, "that" and "and," serve as a guide for designing advanced and differentiated products and allow students to show their complex, in-depth, or abstract understanding of a discipline. Text box 2.1 provides sentence stems you can use to apply "that" and "and" to create criteria (Stambaugh, 2013).

How do you come up with product ideas? Refer back to the criteria for products in Table 1.1. What do experts in the specific discipline create? Begin there. You can also peruse your content standards and determine which standards require a product that students need to create (e.g., timeline, experiment, opinion piece, claim or argument). Most grade-level standards include process and product requirements. Next, combine that product standard with specific criteria from a wheel, depth question, or concept generalization. If, for example, a social studies standard requires that students create a timeline, you can use "that" and "and"' by asking students to create a timeline (standards) "that" incorporates two different relationships on the Social Studies Wheel (complexity) "and" also incorporates a concept or generalization (abstractness). So, your product with criteria, after applying a sentence stem from Text box 2.1 might be "Create a timeline that shows the interaction between the social and political events that occurred after 9/11 and show how those events contributed to the later conflict."

Make sure that you are not just listing a set of criteria. The "that' and "and" stems should include interactions among variables, debatable questions with evaluation options, or concept connections. A misuse of "that" and "and" criteria follows: "Write a story that includes two characters and a city setting." In this instance there are no interactions, depth questions, or concepts included. It is just a checkbox of what to include – a story with two characters and a setting. Instead, we could use a Fictional Writing Wheel and complexity features (interactions; see Appendix A3) as well as concepts (abstractness) to complete a story. An intended use of the criteria would then be: "Write a story that shows how the main character adjusts to (or interacts with) a change in setting and promotes the theme of bravery." Additional examples for applying the stems in multiple content areas and differentiation features previously discussed are found in Table 2.8. Products can also be differentiated or scaffolded down by omitting the "and." In the previous narrative writing example, you could delete the requirement of the theme of bravery and simply require an interaction between characters and setting.

Differentiation as Part of Lesson Design

Differentiation through acceleration, depth, complexity, and abstractness can occur within individual lessons or as part of an overall unit design and is dependent upon student interest, experience, and readiness for specific tasks. You can organize a unit around a depth question or specific generalizations

Text box 2.1

Stems for adding criteria:
- Create a _____ that _____ and _____.
- Design a _____ that shows how _____ and _____ interact to _____.
- Solve _____ by designing a _____ that _____ and _____.

TABLE 2.8 Differentiated product examples with criteria

Product Example without Criteria	Product Example with Criteria	Differentiation Features
Create a skit that shows the conflict in chapter 3 of the story.	Create a skit *that* shows the interaction between the setting *and* the conflict and explain how those interactions help us understand the theme.	Complexity is added using the Literary Analysis Wheel interactions as the skit must show the interaction between setting, conflict, and theme.
Create a model that shows a food web in your area.	Create a model *that* shows what would happen if one element of the food web were eliminated *and* how that elimination impacts the system over time.	Abstractness is added using the universal theme and generalization of systems. The model must show how elements of the food web interact, including demonstrating a generalization of systems (when one element changes the other parts of the system responds).
Solve this problem: (4+9) – (7 x 4) Explain how the use of parentheses impact the solution.	Create as many solutions as possible *that* use two sets of parentheses to arrive at different responses *and* show how the use of parentheses follows a pattern that allows for prediction.	Abstractness is added by asking students to determine multiple solutions and to justify a generalization about patterns.
Dress up like your selected person from your state and create a speech that outlines how your person contributed to your state's development.	Dress up like your selected person and create a speech *that* explains from your person's perspective how geography, social structure, and world events contributed to your person's success *and* led to their notoriety.	Complexity is added by using interactions on the Social Studies Wheel to discuss the contributions of the person's notoriety.
Write an essay that explains the theme of the story.	Write a persuasive essay *that* answers the question "Is this story more about bravery or redemption?" *and* shows how at least three different literary elements interact to support your claim.	Depth and complexity are added. Depth is added by asking students to decide between two different ideas; complexity is added by asking students to examine interactions among multiple literary elements on the wheel.

and embed accelerated content with content wheels and specific and authentic products based on criteria. See the final section of Chapter 8 for an example of a differentiated and interdisciplinary unit design that applies the differentiation features and models discussed in this chapter to ELA and science. Here, we show an example (see Figure 2.4) of an individual lesson and text prompt that incorporate the features of depth, complexity, and abstractness using the poem, "Wild Swans at Coole" by Yeats as a prompt.

Differentiated Feature	Application	Explanation
Standard	CCSS.ELA-LITERACY.RL.7.4 Determine the meaning of words and phrases as they are used in a text, including figurative and connotative meanings; analyze the impact of rhymes and other repetitions of sounds (e.g., alliteration) on a specific verse or stanza of a poem or section of a story or drama. Differentiated Standard: Analyze how historical context and author's purpose contributed to the use of words and phrases as they are used in the text (including figurative and connotative meanings) and their impact on other literary features; analyze the impact of rhymes and other repetitions of sounds on a specific verse or stanza of a poem or section of a story or drama.	Standard is differentiated by complexity. The example shows the contribution of additional elements (historical context and author's purpose) on the use of words, phrases, and figurative meanings.
Depth	Forced-choice question: Is this poem about losing love or growing old?	This forced-choice question can be asked for students to gather evidence to justify one choice or the other as they initially explore what the poem is about. The choice might be further supported by use of the Literary Analysis Wheel. In a quick debate, students can stand on opposite sides of the room to defend their point of view and refer to the text for evidence. Students may also research historical information relevant to W.B. Yeats and the context of the poem to defend their claim.
Complexity	Use of Literary Analysis Wheel Ask students about separate elements first, then ask complex questions that include the interaction of elements. Simple Questions: - Characters: How would you describe the swans? What are their actions? What inferences can you make about their motivations? What inferences can you make about the values of the narrator? - Symbols: What symbols do you notice in the poem? What might the swans symbolize? What is important about the number of swans (nine and fifty swans)? - Tone: How would you describe the tone? Does it shift throughout the poem? Why? Complex Questions: - Symbol + Conflict: How does the symbolism of the swans help us understand the narrator's conflict? - Context + Theme: How does the context contribute to the interpretation of the theme?	The Literary Analysis Wheel is used as a model to explicitly teach the function of literary elements within an integrated whole. In this way, students can start to develop the interpretation skills of a literary scholar.

FIGURE 2.4 Lesson planning with differentiation features: ELA literature poem, "Wild Swans at Coole" by Yeats

Abstractness	Ask students to complete the Big Idea Reflection. Students may also respond to a question about power such as "How does the concept of power relate to the poem" (e.g., time is a powerful influence)	Students identify concepts, understand the importance of these concepts, and consider the implications of these concepts as they relate to their lives. Understanding how ideas in the poem relate to real-world contexts allows students to interpret literature as a reflection of the human experience.
Differentiated Task	Grade-Level Task: Create a poem movie that shows the theme of the poem in "The Wild Swans at Coole." Use images to convey the mood, setting, and important symbols in the poem. Differentiated: Is the poem about beginnings or endings? Create a poem movie that defends your point of view by conveying how the setting, structure, language, and symbolism contribute to developing this idea. Use images as symbolic representations for various symbols (e.g., swans, a still sky, woodland paths) as they relate to the historical context and author's purpose.	The task incorporates depth with a forced-choice question that requires a high-level analysis of the poem. It is a more generalized question than the original depth question (Is the poem about losing love or growing old?), allowing for more applied abstract thinking. Complexity is included through the interaction of multiple literary elements. Overall, students justify the depth question by applying the thinking of a literary scholar in order to communicate a sophisticated analysis for an audience. Note the task aligns with the standard. The use of the Literary Analysis Wheel prepares the student to accomplish this task.

FIGURE 2.4 (Cont.)

Conclusion

This chapter serves as an overview of definitions and frameworks for differentiating instruction through a talent-development lens. The models discussed support students in developing expertise and preparing them for creative productivity in a field of interest and strength as they develop their potential. Additionally, the models, frameworks, and strategies highlighted throughout this book align with the National Association for Gifted Children's (NAGC) Programming Standards for Curriculum and Instruction and can be used, in part, to support NAGC's Teacher Preparation Standards in curriculum and instruction. The chapters that follow apply the definitions and frameworks previously outlined to content-specific disciplines. Multiple examples are given to guide your thinking and application to your own setting. The definitions and models outlined here can be used as a springboard for creating common language about differentiation for academically advanced students. The models and frameworks discussed here have been piloted in a variety of schools. Teachers report a deeper understanding of how to differentiate and find that the models provide them with a guide for differentiating instruction for academically advanced students with confidence. Student pre-post data show positive learning gains in content acquisition and a students' ability to determine interactions, defend ideas, and connect newly learned ideas to abstract generalizations and concepts.

3

Models for Differentiating Instruction in English Language Arts – Literature

In the study of language arts, students essentially study how language is crafted to convey meaning. Students analyze literary elements, identify the main idea and supporting details, and differentiate facts from opinions. Such skills are foundational for a solid understanding of language, its use, and its function. However, to put students on a trajectory toward expertise in language arts, we must intentionally guide students to develop an integrated knowledge structure of how to think about the language arts. Literary scholars have expertise in applying in-depth analysis in understanding how parts of language work together to create meaning and interpret that meaning through a lens such as formalism, historicism, archetypal patterns, or other forms of literary theory. While most school-aged children do not typically engage in formal literary criticism to analyze texts, we can begin to provide the mental frameworks that help students begin to recognize patterns, structures, and relationships in the way experts do.

In this chapter, we provide examples of how to use models for analyzing and interpreting texts that begin to foster expertise. We show how the differentiation features of complexity, depth, and abstractness can be applied to questioning, tasks, and products within ELA so that students have opportunities to think as an expert and internalize processes inherent to the discipline.

Instructional Ideas and Models for Adding Complexity in ELA Literature

Adding complexity to a text in ELA promotes students' understanding of how different text features in a story, poem, or video interact in ways that support the theme or an interpretation. The Literary Analysis Wheel – Primary (intended for students in K-3; Appendix A2) and the Literary Analysis Wheel (intended for students Grades 3–12; Appendix A2), shown next, support this thinking by combining the different literary elements so that students determine how their interactions promote meaning.

Before applying an in-depth analysis, allow students to read the text and check for basic comprehension and understanding of unknown vocabulary (if needed). Then introduce students to the Literary Analysis Wheel and begin asking simple questions first (one element on the wheel), recording appropriate responses and then moving to more complex questions and interactions (how one element contributes to, interacts with, or impacts another). It is important to help students see the connections visually by drawing arrows among multiple elements of the wheel to indicate relationships. It is not necessary to explicitly teach all components of the wheel before analyzing a text. If students are unfamiliar with alliteration or similes, for example, take a moment to teach that content and continue the analysis.

Once students become accustomed to using the Literary Analysis Wheel, they can use it as a tool to plan their own narrative writing. They can consider how their purpose and theme influence the way they develop their characters, establish the setting throughout the story, use style to develop tone, etc. By going beyond a typical storyboard approach in which students plan plot sequence and character interactions, the wheel allows students to understand how literary elements contribute to each other to create overall meaning. Students may also use the Fictional Writing Wheel in similar ways as shown with the Literary Analysis Wheel to plan for narrative writing. An example of the Fictional Writing Wheel can be found in Appendix A3.

Younger Student Example: Literary Analysis Wheel – Primary (K-3): "The Man, the Boy, and the Donkey" by Aesop
After students have an initial understanding of the text, lead students through completion of the Literary Analysis Wheel – Primary, first by asking simple questions about each element, then by asking complex questions (how one element contributes to, interacts with, or impacts another). See Figure 3.1 for an example of how elements of the wheel connect across elements.

Simple Questions for Beginning Discussion and Modeling
The following are examples of simple questions to ask in guiding an initial discussion about the text.

- Use of Words/Techniques: What words in the story are important to understand? Why? (Students may pick out words like shame, lazy, and jeer, and talk about why those words are important.)
- Feelings of the Author (Tone) and Reader (Mood): What feelings do you get from reading this text? (Perhaps surprise that the Man and the boy raised the pole and Donkey on their shoulders; shock that the Donkey drowned)
- Sequence/Plot: Retell the story in four sentences: First, Then, Next, and Finally. . . .
- Conflict/Problem: What is the main problem in the story? (The Man and the boy need to get to the market, but others criticize them.)
- Structure and Style: Why might the only words in quotations in the story be that of the country and townspeople? (To show the ridicule of others; only the voices of the townspeople are heard instead of the voices of the man and the boy.)
- Setting: How does the setting change over the course of the story? (Countryside to town)
- Characters: What is the significance of the Man and his son as the main characters of the story? (An older and younger person – maybe one is supposed to be wiser than the other)
- Point of View: From which point of view is the story told? (Narrator-Third person)

Complex Questions for Discussion and Differentiation
The following are examples of complex questions.

- Plot + Character: How does the Man change at each interaction with the townspeople? (The Man keeps changing his mind based on new influences.)
- Point of View + Character: How does the point of view (third person) impact how the reader interacts with the characters? How might readers interpret the story if told from the townspeople? The Man or the Boy? (The reader is able to know what the townspeople, Man, and Boy are thinking. If this were told from the Man's perspective or the townspeople's perspective (first person) then we may not fully understand the conflict.)
- Sequence/Plot + Setting + Conflict: How does the sequence of the story and the setting help readers understand the Man and the Boy's dilemma?

Synthesis of All Elements

The following questions can be used to guide students in synthesizing the overall meaning of the text.

- Theme: In this fable, the theme is provided for you (Please all, and you will please none). How is it supported by the other elements on the wheel? (The end of the story shows the extreme consequence of the donkey drowning – we lose our very treasures when we try to please others. The third-person narrator helps us observe this lesson unfold through the conflict of man vs. society.)
- Interpretation: Taken altogether, how do you interpret and interact with the fable? (Student responses vary depending on how they relate to the ideas. Students might note they interpret this as a caution not to change in response to others' opinions.)

Older Student Example: Literary Analysis Wheel (Intermediate and Middle/Early High School): "The Wild Swans at Coole" by W.B. Yeats

Before applying an in-depth analysis, students first need to understand the text they are reading. It may be necessary to guide students through some basic comprehension questions or paraphrasing of stanzas. You may also need to provide background information on the poem to aid in interpretation (written in Ireland after World War I). After students have an initial understanding of the text, lead students through completion of the Literary Analysis Wheel, first by asking simple questions

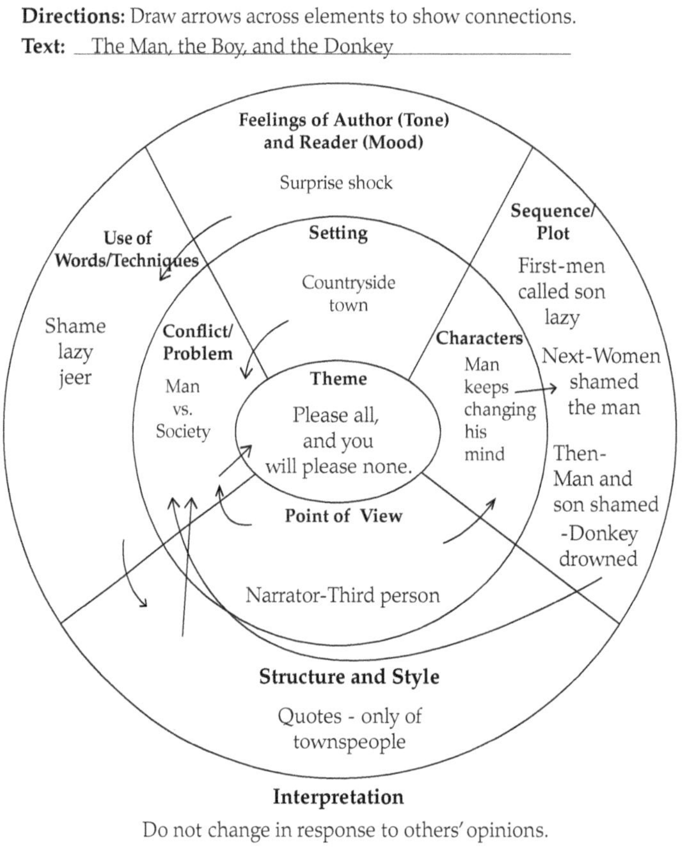

Directions: Draw arrows across elements to show connections.
Text: The Man, the Boy, and the Donkey

[Literary Analysis Wheel diagram with the following elements:]

- Feelings of Author (Tone) and Reader (Mood): Surprise shock
- Setting: Countryside town
- Sequence/Plot: First-men called son lazy; Next-Women shamed the man; Then-Man and son shamed -Donkey drowned
- Characters: Man keeps changing his mind
- Theme: Please all, and you will please none.
- Conflict/Problem: Man vs. Society
- Use of Words/Techniques: Shame lazy jeer
- Point of View: Narrator-Third person
- Structure and Style: Quotes - only of townspeople
- Interpretation: Do not change in response to others' opinions.

FIGURE 3.1 Example of completed Literary Analysis – Primary Wheel – "The Man, the Boy, and the Donkey" – Aesop

about each element, then by asking complex questions (how one element contributes to, interacts with, or impacts another).

Simple Questions for Beginning Discussion and Modeling
The following are examples of simple questions to ask in guiding an initial discussion about the text.

- Setting: What is the setting of the poem? (Autumn, twilight, by a pond at Coole)
- Characters: How would you describe the swans? What are their actions? What inferences can you make about their motivations? What inferences can you make about the values of the narrator? (The swans are beautiful and mysterious – brimming among the still water; the narrator treasures his time watching the swans year after year.)
- Symbols: What symbols do you notice in the poem? What might the swans symbolize? What is important about the number of swans (Nine and fifty swans)? (The swans represent an ideal – something beautiful and perfect. Swans are monogamous, one swan is missing, symbolizing the idea of loss.)
- Mood: How would you describe the mood? (Nostalgic, longing)
- Language/Style/Structure: What figurative language do you notice in the poem? ("wander where they will" – alliteration; note the structure of the rhyme scheme ABCBDD and rhythm is roughly iambic.)
- Plot/Conflict: What is the major conflict for the narrator? (The narrator is upset that the swans are flying away.)
- Tone: How would you describe the tone? Does it shift throughout the poem? Why? (The tone begins as peaceful and plaintive, then to admiring, then to regretful.)
- Point of View: From what point of view is the poem written? (Narrator-third person limited of the speaker)
- Purpose/Context: What do you think Yeats's purpose is for writing the poem? What is the context? (Ireland has undergone a huge amount of change since the beginning of World War I. Yeats also proposed to a woman for marriage but was rejected. Yeats's purpose may be to express the aching feelings associated with change.)

Complex Questions for Discussion and Differentiation
The following are examples of complex questions.

- Setting + Symbol: How does the setting in the poem serve as a symbol? (The setting of autumn and twilight are symbols of change. Something is ending.)
- Symbol + Character: Why does the author emphasize mirrors and reflection? How does this symbolism help us understand the narrator? (The symbolism allows us to see that he is contemplating his own life through the admiration of the ideal swans. The swans, representing an "ideal" are unwearied. His heart, by contrast, is "sore" because this "ideal" is coming to an end. The mirrors allow us to see his contemplation of something ending – perhaps his youth, he is losing a love, or that things are changing.)
- Tone + Language: How does the author's use of language help establish the tone and shifts in tone? (The use of the words autumn beauty in the first stanza creates a positive tone. In the third stanza, the words "now my heart is sore" shifts the tone, then to positive admiration with the words – "companionable" and "passion," then to regret with the final question.)
- Language + Character: What language does the author use to describe the swans? How does this help us understand the narrator's values? (The swans are described as "mysterious,"

"beautiful," and "unwearied." This helps us understand that the narrator values observing the swans year after year and helps us understand his sadness about them flying away.)
- Symbol + Theme: How does the symbolism of the swans help us understand the message of the poem? (The idea that one swan is missing helps us understand the theme relates to change or losing an ideal. The mirror helps us understand that the narrator is contemplating these ideas.)

Synthesis of All Elements
- Theme: After analyzing the elements of the poem, what is the theme? (Appreciate the present, Change/Growing old/Losing an ideal can be difficult)
- Interpretation: Taken altogether, how do you interpret and interact with the poem? (Student responses vary depending on how they relate to the ideas in the poem. For example, middle school students are facing the change of leaving their childhood).

Creating Complex and Differentiated Questions Using the Literary Analysis Wheel

The Literary Analysis Wheel provides a framework for thinking about how the elements interact to develop the theme of a poem, short story, or novel. It can also be used as a tool to differentiate questions, tasks, and assignments. In addition to teaching the wheel as indicated previously, you can design tiered questions that are deliberately differentiated toward increased complexity. The wheel is used to create questions that could be assigned to various groups based on their level of understanding or as a way to increasingly add more rigorous discussions in the classroom.

As shown in Table 3.1, Level 1 questions focus on understanding single elements on the wheel. Level 2 questions focus on interactions between two different elements on the wheel, and Level 3 questions combine three elements or encourage divergent thinking by asking students to manipulate elements on the wheel and discuss alternatives. When possible, add specificity from the text into the questions (e.g., how does the landscape of the countryside influence the perceptions of the characters?) as opposed to simply asking a question using category names from the wheel (e.g., how does the setting influence the conflict?).

Creating Complex and Differentiated Tasks

In addition to asking leveled questions, you can use the Literary Analysis Wheel to create differentiated and complex tasks and activities. Begin by plotting where the typical assignment might fit on the wheel (i.e., which section or element does the grade-level task fit) and then add another element or interaction to the task. We provide several examples in Table 3.2 of grade-level tasks differentiated with complexity. Note that the task demands do not require students to discuss multiple and isolated

TABLE 3.1 Questions with increased levels of complexity: ELA Literature

Increasing Levels of Complexity	*Example of Differentiated Questions for "The Man, the Boy, and the Donkey" by Aesop*	*Example Questions for "Wild Swans at Coole" by W.B. Yeats*
Level 1: A single element	What do we know about the man's character?	What is the setting in the poem? What is the main problem for the narrator?
Level 2: Interaction of elements	How do the events in the story (plot) influence the man's thoughts and behaviors (character)?	How does the author's use of alliteration "wander where they will" affect the mood of the poem?
Level 3: Manipulate elements and consider the possibilities or combine interactions among multiple elements	How might the theme of the story be different if the story were told from the townspeople's perspective?	What if the poem were written from the swan's point of view? How would this affect the author's word choice, tone shifts, and overall meaning?

TABLE 3.2 Examples of differentiated complex tasks in ELA Literature

Grade-Level Task Example	Task Differentiated with Complexity Using the Wheel Elements to Add Complexity
Create a new ending to the story that includes the same theme.	Create a new ending to the story that includes symbolism as a way to develop the theme of individuality.
What questions would you ask the author to better understand the poem? What would you want to know about the author's purpose?	What questions would you ask the author about his/her purpose in writing the poem? How would the understanding of purpose and context guide your interpretation of symbols and tone within the poem?
Explain the plot using evidence from the text. Make a diagram labeling the significant events.	Explain how the plot events caused change in character behaviors and interactions with other characters. Make a diagram to show these interactions and how they change the character.
Create a monologue from the perspective of a minor character that shows his thoughts regarding his/her relationship with the main character.	Create a monologue from the perspective of a minor character that shows his/her internal conflict and how this influences the relationship with the main character and propels the rising action.
Bring in four objects that symbolically represent significant ideas in the poem.	Bring in four objects that symbolically represent how the mood and point of view interact to support the theme.
Develop a soundtrack choosing ten songs for the book. Use appropriate songs to match the events and mood within the book and explain with textual evidence why these songs relate to the book.	Develop a soundtrack choosing ten songs for the book. Analyze the lyrics and show how the song writer uses techniques (alliteration, similes, symbols) to help listeners understand the main idea of the song, then relate the main idea of the song to the book.

elements of the wheel in succession but require students to think about the *interactions* between and among the elements.

Essentially you are differentiating the criteria of the task demand by asking students to examine more complex relationships that support a richer understanding of a text. The wheels serve both as a planning tool for teachers and as a learning guide for students; teachers can use the wheel as a guide for creating complex tasks while students use the wheel to respond to the tasks presented after discussion.

Depth

Applying depth to an ELA curriculum can be accomplished by asking carefully designed debatable questions. These questions may come in the form of "should" or "forced-choice" questions that require students to form an opinion with supporting evidence, justify a stance, conduct additional research to craft a response, or examine various possibilities, perspectives, and scenarios. In ELA, evidential support is derived from the texts they read and the inferences they are making about those texts. Once the question is designed, students form an educated opinion or position based on the evidence and data (i.e., fiction or nonfiction texts and other resources available). Depth questions are not intended to be judgment-based queries that lack textual or other evidential support but larger, real-world questions that encourage students to form an opinion by interpreting textual evidence and drawing conclusions based on their own research or analysis.

An example of a depth question for the story, "The Man, the Boy, and the Donkey" by Aesop could be "Were the Man and the Boy victims of other people's rudeness or their own self-doubt?" This question encourages students to examine the text, make inferences, and form an opinion that is justifiable from the story based on their individual interpretation or research. Similarly, for the poem, "The Wild

Swans at Coole," the debatable (forced-choice) question "Is this poem about losing lost love or growing older?" allows students to use evidence from the text (and evidence from the Literary Analysis Wheel) to justify their argument.

Depth questions prompt students to engage with content deeply in order to sufficiently support their response. In exploring the depth question, students think as experts and figure out what they know and don't know to answer the question. Students can use elements of the wheel as a way to uncover content that would substantiate a claim. For example, students consider, "What do I know about this element (e.g., setting)? How does this support or refute a claim?" For example, while answering "Is the poem about losing lost love or growing older" from "The Wild Swans at Coole," they use the thinking skills of a literary scholar to consider how the elements of symbolism, setting, and tone support losing lost love or growing older. Students may also want to conduct biographical research on Yeats' life and the historical context of when and where the poem was written to further justify their arguments.

Overarching Depth Questions

Debatable questions can be posed that would require multiple lessons, texts, or resources throughout a larger unit of study. In order to answer the question, students explore multiple points of view from various texts or media. For example, an overarching question for a unit might be, "Does your environment change your identity?" Students answer the question by forming an opinion and providing evidence for their ideas and individual interpretations. Table 3.3 shows examples of how art and short stories might be used to explore this question through multiple perspectives. After examining this question through multiple texts, students write an opinion piece that incorporates examples from the three selected texts and their own research. This adds complexity through the examination of interactions among various elements and interactions among different stories and art selections (i.e., different perspectives). Depth questions are useful especially for facilitating Socratic seminars or providing an overarching question for examining the multiple texts.

Depth Applied to Standards and Tasks

Questions that promote depth can be applied across all reading genres and disciplines. Debatable questions support the integration of multiple standards. When integrating standards with a depth question, you can combine a reading standard with a writing or speaking and listening standard. The

TABLE 3.3 Overarching depth question for unit

Does your environment change your identity?		
"All Summer in a Day" – Ray Bradbury	*"Dark They Were and Golden-Eyed" – Ray Bradbury*	*"Day and Night" – M.C. Escher (Art)*
No – even in a new environment, Margot continued to maintain her core self, even when she was made fun of. This is revealed through plot elements (students make fun of her for being different) and characterization.	Yes – even though Mr. Bittering was resistant to changing, his change was a result of a slow progression of letting go of his dreams. This is portrayed through his characterization and symbolism (rusting rocket, changing of eyes, etc.)	Can be argued either way, based on the observer's interpretation of the art.
Write an opinion piece that answers the question, "Does your environment change your identity?" Incorporate examples from at least three different short story or art pieces we have done in class as well as your own research. Be sure to provide specific textual examples to support your opinion.		

Source: Adapted from Mofield & Stambaugh (2016a). Prufrock Press. Used with permission.

Models for Differentiating Instruction in English Language Arts – Literature ◆ 27

TABLE 3.4 Depth tied to standards and tasks in ELA literature

Depth (Debatable) Question	Product or Activity and Standard	Reading Standard	Specific Task Demand
Is Jack greedy? (from "Jack and the Beanstalk")	Socratic Seminar Discussion CCSS.ELA-LITERACY.SL.1.1.B Build on others' talk in conversations by responding to the comments of others through multiple exchanges.	CCSS.ELA-LITERACY.RL.1.1 Ask and answer questions about key details in a text.	During a Socratic seminar, students build on each other's ideas to develop conclusions about Jack's character based on evidence from the text.
Is Meg a hero? (*A Wrinkle in Time*)	Persuasive Essay CCSS.ELA-LITERACY.W.6.1 Write arguments to support claims with clear reasons and relevant evidence.	CCSS.ELA-LITERACY.RL.6.3 Describe how a particular story's or drama's plot unfolds in a series of episodes as well as how the characters respond or change as the plot moves toward a resolution.	Is Meg a hero? Justify your stance in a persuasive essay, citing relevant evidence from the text that includes specific and detailed examples from the text about Meg and her quest.
Is the poem relevant to today?	Quick Debate CCSS.ELA-LITERACY.SL.8.1.D Acknowledge new information expressed by others, and, when warranted, qualify or justify their own views in light of the evidence presented.	CCSS.ELA-LITERACY.RL.8.1 Cite the textual evidence that most strongly supports an analysis of what the text says explicitly as well as inferences drawn from the text.	Students stand on opposite sides of the room to defend their point of view.
Should the character choose ___ or ___ ?	Create a T-chart using evidence to support both choices. CCSS.ELA-LITERACY.W.4.5 With guidance and support from peers and adults, develop and strengthen writing as needed by planning, revising, and editing.	CCSS.ELA-LITERACY.RL.4.3 Describe in depth a character, setting, or event in a story or drama, drawing on specific details in the text (e.g., a character's thoughts, words, or actions).	As a pre-writing planning activity, students create a chart to show the positive and negative implications of the character's decision.

Should or Debatable Question Should the Man and the Boy listen to the villagers?			
Character's Purpose or Goal Get the donkey to the market			
Choice 1 Listen to the villagers and keep changing the plan		Choice 2 Make up your own mind and perhaps be made fun of	
Assumption The villagers know better what to do		Assumption The Man and the Boy know better what to do	
Evidence/Inference The villagers in each town had a different idea about what to do based on their perspective (Ask students to cite examples that show this)		Evidence/Inference They were probably going to be made fun of regardless.	
Positive Implications (short and long-term)	Negative Implications (short and long-term)	Positive Implications (short and long-term)	Negative Implications (short and long-term)
You keep others happy by doing what they want you to do.	Short term gain for long term pain. You may lose yourself or lose sight of your goal if you listen to others who may not know you.	You learn perseverance and independent thinking. Even though you get made fun of, in the end it works out well for you and you reach your goal.	You choose short term pain for long term gain; you get made fun of by others who disagree with you.
What other criteria, questions, or information should be considered to achieve the purpose or goal? When do I listen to others and when do I follow my own thoughts and ideas?			

FIGURE 3.2 Choice Reasoning Chart – Humanities: "The Man, the Boy, and the Donkey"

writing or speaking and listening standards dictate the product selection while the reading standard provides guidelines for answering the questioning using the specific criteria required in a standard. The combination of multiple standards into one larger task also promotes complexity. As emphasized in Chapter 2, standards may also be accelerated for advanced learners as well as the readings and resources. Table 3.4 shows several examples of how depth can be incorporated with several ELA standards and task demands.

Depth: Choice-Reasoning Chart

The Choice-Reasoning Chart – Humanities (see Appendix B1) provides a structure for students to apply elements of critical thinking as they make decisions about debatable questions (Paul & Elder, 2019). As students reason through a question, they first think through their purpose. From here, various choices can be considered. Beyond thinking through each choice, students can examine underlying assumptions (e.g., values and beliefs), the evidence and inferences considered with each choice, along with the positive and negative implications of each choice. This structure allows students to make more sophisticated judgments in constructing arguments, going beyond simply justifying choices with evidence. Figure 3.2 shows an example of the Choice Reasoning Chart – Humanities applied to "The Man, the Boy, and the Donkey."

Abstractness

Concept Maps and Organizers

Abstractness is the connection of facts to broader ideas such as generalizations, rules, theories, concepts, laws, or principles. The incorporation of abstractness in ELA can be achieved in a variety of

Generalizations for Adding Abstractness	Textual Evidence from" The Man and the Donkey" by Aesop
Power can be used or abused.	The Man and the Boy abused the power they had over themselves because they tried to please everyone else.
Power is connected to a source.	The source of power in the story was the townspeople and their words. The Man and the Boy allowed the townspeople to have power over them by listening to and doing what they said.
Power is the ability to influence.	The townspeople used their words to exert power over the Man and the Boy. The Man and the Boy did not use their power to influence their own thinking and life.
Connection to another concept Power + _____	Power + Change: People have the power to change themselves and others.

FIGURE 3.3 Concept Organizer: "The Man, the Boy, and the Donkey"

ways. You can introduce specific generalizations to students and ask them to connect ideas from a text to those generalizations as indicated in Figure 3.3. A more detailed explanation and examples of generalizations is found in Chapter 2. Concept maps (see Chapter 2) are another effective tool for encouraging students to organize their ideas and amass facts into broader categories and specific generalizations. In this way students are not just discussing concepts on a general level but supporting specific generalizations with evidence from a variety of sources.

Figure 3.3 shows an example of adding abstractness to the fable "The Man, the Boy, and the Donkey." Students complete the concept organizer explaining how the fable supports different generalizations about power. Students can continue to add to this handout as it applies to other stories or texts.

Abstractness and the Big Idea Reflection

The Big Idea Reflection (see Appendix C2) is a way for students to think about concepts within a text, how those concepts relate to each other, and how those concepts apply to students' lives. This framework allows the students to consider the major ideas about the human experience that are captured within a piece of literature and then consider how these concepts relate to broad generalizations, issues in the current world, and students themselves. This is especially important to the discipline of language arts. Literature communicates ideas about life: problems, celebrations, successes, failures, accompanying emotions, and relevant culture. The Big Idea Reflection helps students recognize these ideas in a way that integrates the content with the learner.

Students may need guidance in understanding what is meant by an abstract concept. It may be useful to explain that these concepts are ideas that cannot be seen, heard, or touched. Provide students with examples such as "change, power, order, structure, freedom, sacrifice, hope, etc."

Another approach for incorporating abstractness is to provide a list of concept words that relate to the text. For example, from "The Man, the Boy, and the Donkey," the word list might be conformity, self-doubt, change, individuality, influence, and disappointment. This concept list serves as a word bank in which students create sentences using at least two of these words that capture a major idea or message in the story. Students may write "Conformity can lead to disappointment" or "Self-doubt can influence conformity" to convey a big idea that generalizes beyond the text.

Figure 3.4 shows an example of student responses for the Big Idea Reflection applied to "The Wild Swans at Coole."

What	**Concepts** What concepts/ideas are in the text?	nostalgia, regret, love, change, appreciation of past and present
	Generalizations What broad statement can you make about one or more of these concepts? Make it generalizable beyond the text.	Change allows for appreciation of the past and present.
So What	**Issue** What is the main issue, problem, or conflict?	Saying goodbye to something you hold dear; Confronting a major change in your life
	Insight on Life What insight on life is provided from this text?	The "ideal, flawless" things in our life will eventually go away; change is a part of our lives . . . youth, beauty, childhood, family, love; "Don't cry because it's over, smile because it happened"- Dr. Seuss
	World-Community-Individual How does this text relate to you, your community, or your world? What question does the author want you to ask yourself?	Individual- what are the flawless ideals I want to hold on to in my life? Will they change? How can I spend my time in the most valuable ways today? Peers- Students may connect by realizing they are saying goodbye to childhood or middle school if moving on to high school. World- The United States is not the same after 9-11 terrorist attacks- this relates to Yeats's ideas of Ireland changing
Now What	**Implications** How should you respond to the ideas in the text? What action should you take? What are the implications of the text? What can you do with this information?	What can I do to prepare for upcoming changes in my own life? What must I consider about the present before it is gone?

Note. Adapted from Mofield, E., & Stambaugh, T. (2016b). *Perspectives of power: ELA lessons for gifted and advanced learners in grades 6-8*. Prufrock Press. Used with permission.

FIGURE 3.4 Big Idea Reflection – "The Wild Swans at Coole"

Checking for Understanding

If we teach in a way that encourages higher-level thinking and expert thinking, then the tasks and activities that we ask students to complete need to mirror the instruction. Otherwise, how will we be sure that students understand the information presented? So, the tasks, products, and activities are also differentiated by applying depth, complexity, or abstractness in ways that mimic the more advanced instructional tasks and daily activities.

You can provide a more rigorous task for students by incorporating more than one differentiation feature. As noted in Table 3.5, the grade-level tasks are differentiated by including depth and complexity, complexity and abstractness, or abstractness and depth. This combination allows students to practice multiple applications of expert thinking within the task. Consider a student's readiness and pace of learning when considering the extent to which differentiation features are applied. Of course, content can also be differentiated by substituting the reading level of the story or the concepts and inferences required.

TABLE 3.5 Differentiated and advanced tasks with differentiation features: ELA literature examples

Grade-Level Task	Differentiated and Advanced Task	Applicable Features of Differentiation
Draw an illustration of the book that conveys the setting. Use important details from the book.	Draw an illustration of the book to convey how the setting creates the mood. Explain how the illustration supports the idea "discovery leads to discovery."	Includes abstractness by incorporating the concept of "discovery." Includes complexity by including how setting creates the mood.
Create a movie trailer of your book that will encourage others to read your book. Be sure to highlight the literary features.	Do obstacles make us stronger? Create a movie trailer for your book that conveys how characters in the book might respond to this question. Within your movie trailer, showcase how various conflicts shape the plot, creating suspense for the viewer to want to read the book.	Includes depth by including a debatable question that requires substantive support. Includes complexity by adding the interaction of conflict and plot.
From the perspective of the main character, write a narrative that explains how your relationship with another character changed over time. Use evidence from the story to convey your feelings.	Should you trust your friend after they hurt you? From the perspective of the main character, write a narrative that answers the question based on your experiences with another character. Craft your narrative with word connotations that develop a tone that conveys your feelings.	Includes depth as a debatable question. Includes complexity by adding the interaction of language, style, and tone.
Make a storyboard that shows the sequence of events within the story "The Man, the Boy, and the Donkey." Include the problem and how it is resolved.	Make a storyboard that shows the sequence of events within the story "The Man, the Boy, and the Donkey" to show how "encounters lead to opportunities and threats." Label how character encounters lead to conflicts and how these conflicts are resolved by characters' actions.	Includes abstractness by asking students to support "encounters lead to opportunities and threats." Includes complexity with the interaction of character, conflict, and plot.
Write a review of your book on a blog post that encourages others to read your book.	Write a review of your book on a blog post that relates the ideas of the book to the concept of "identity." In the blog, explain how the character's actions, motives, and values influence the mood for the reader.	Includes abstractness by relating the blog to "identity." Includes complexity with the interaction of character and mood.
Create a poem movie to show the theme of the poem "The Wild Swans at Coole." Use images to convey the mood, setting, and important symbols in the poem.	Is the poem "The Wild Swans at Coole" about beginnings or endings? Create a poem movie that defends your point of view by conveying how the setting, structure, language, and symbolism contribute to "beginnings" or "endings." Use images as symbolic representations for various symbols (e.g., swans, mirrors a still sky, woodland paths) as they relate to the historical context and author's purpose.	Includes depth with a forced-choice question. Includes complexity with the interaction of multiple elements.

Book Project Choices with Differentiation Features

These ideas for ELA are popular projects that are often given to grade-level students, but they have been differentiated with complexity, depth, and/or abstractness in order to provide more challenge.

- Create a movie trailer for the book (2–3 minutes). In your video trailer, be sure to show the character's values, motivations, and what the character is learning about life through conflicts. Show examples of how "change leads to conflict and conflict leads to change."
- Create an alternate ending to the book (in video or story form). Show how the new ending affects the theme of the story and how encounters in the new ending led to new possible threats and opportunities.
- Create a chapter that might proceed Chapter 1 (in video or story form). Reveal insight into the main character's thoughts, feelings, and actions. Use symbolism as a foreshadowing device for future plot events. Write the chapter to help the reader understand "Does the character shape their experience or does their experience shape the character?"
- Create a soundtrack list for the book. Include at least five songs and provide an explanation of what part of the plot each song goes with. Also, explain how each song relates to a generalization about truth (e.g., perception of truth varies; there are positives and negatives to realizing truth, there are consequences to believing perception rather than truth). What is the significance of the generalization through the character's journey?
- Create a soundtrack list for a character in the book. Include at least five songs and provide an explanation of how the song demonstrates qualities of the character. Explain the significance of how specific lyrics relate to specific aspects of the character and what aspects of the story (interactions with characters, internal conflicts, etc.) caused the character to show these qualities or emotions. Then answer, "Is the character a rebel or a hero?" from various character perspectives.
- Make a list of at least eight symbolic representations to reveal literary elements of the book. Describe what the element represents and how it contributes to another literary element in the story (use the Literary Analysis Wheel to think of connections). (Do not choose obvious symbols such as an apple represents the apple in the story.) For example, a rubber band represents the flexibility displayed by the character throughout specific instances in the book. White out represents how the character is always involved in fixing his mistakes, etc. Include textual evidence from your book to support each symbol. Explain how the idea "power is connected to a source" is related to at least one of your symbolic items.
- Create a monologue from the perspective of a character. In your monologue, reveal your thoughts about the conflict, what you are learning about life, how the setting affects you, and how your interactions with the other characters affect them. Answer "How do encounters with adversity lead to positive and negative changes in you?"
- Think of a major problem in the story. Does the character shape the conflict or the conflict shape the character? Compare the story to two other books or stories noting the patterns between characters and conflicts. Present your comparisons in writing or in video format.

Created by Tamra Stambaugh & Emily Mofield, 2022

Conclusion

The models and ideas within this chapter serve as tools for students to analyze how elements in literature relate to and interact with one another to create cultural, intellectual, or emotional meaning for the reader. These frameworks build a content base for learning about literary elements and provide a structure for recognizing the relationships among them, including their interactions with the author's purpose and the reader's interpretation. On the path toward expertise, students can begin to discern the craft and use of an author's language as a true "art" (language *arts*) conveying meaningful ideas about the world.

4

Models for Differentiating Instruction Using English Language Arts – Informational Texts

To move students toward expertise in ELA beyond interpretation of poetry, short stories, and other literature, it is also important for students to recognize and critically analyze the language, craft, and organization of informational texts. Scholars in the field of English apply sophisticated skills to examine and apply rhetoric to communicate ideas. Though most students do not start applying rhetorical analyses until high school, students can be taught the essential features of rhetoric early on. These skills include learning how to evaluate arguments, analyze how an author develops a central idea, and examine supporting details that support a main idea.

In this chapter, we show how the differentiation features of complexity, depth, and abstractness can be applied to questioning, tasks, and products with ELA informational texts so that students have opportunities to think deeply in ways that promote the habits of an expert and encourage them to internalize processes inherent to the discipline, particularly when reading informational texts.

Instructional Ideas and Models for Adding Complexity in Informational Texts

Adding complexity to a text in ELA promotes students' understanding of how different text features interact in ways that support a main idea, central idea, or claim. This thinking is supported through two different texts and age-specific models (i.e., Text Analysis Wheel – Primary intended for students in K-5; Appendix A4, and the Rhetorical Analysis Wheel, intended for students 6–12; Appendix A5). In this chapter, we provide examples of how these models may be used to add complexity using multiple resources, ages, and readiness levels. These wheels support instruction for the teacher and the learner. For example, you can use the model as a planning guide for differentiating instruction and lesson planning or explicitly teach the model to students as a way to analyze text and internalize expert thinking and inquiry. The specific instructional strategies used depend upon the purpose, classroom context, student readiness levels and prior exposure to this type of thinking and the actual model.

As students become accustomed to using the Text Analysis or Rhetorical Analysis Wheel, they can use it as a tool to plan their own explanatory or argument writing. They can consider how their purpose and claim influences the way they organize their points, establish a logical rationale, and use specific techniques to emphasize information, etc. By going beyond a typical outline approach for pre-planning writing, students using the Argumentative Writing Wheel understand how elements contribute to each other to argue a claim or develop a central idea. An example of the Argumentative Writing Wheel can be found in Appendix A6.

Younger Student Example: Text Analysis Wheel – Primary (K-3): "Pox on You" – Informational Text

Before applying an in-depth analysis, allow students to read the text and check for basic comprehension and understanding of unknown vocabulary (if necessary). Then introduce students to the Text Analysis Wheel – Primary and begin asking simple questions first and recording appropriate responses and then moving to more complex questions and interactions (how one element contributes to, interacts with, or impacts another). It is important to help students see the connections visually by drawing arrows among multiple elements of the wheel to indicate relationships.

A Pox on You!

In medieval times there was no greater curse than to wish "a pox on you and your family." Smallpox was a horrible disease that covered the skin with pus-filled blisters and often killed its victims. Those who survived wore the scars for the rest of their lives. They had circular depressions covering their skin and disfiguring their faces. In severe cases, people lost parts of their lips, ears, and tips of their nose.

The first symptoms were fever, chills, headache, and backache. Then a rash covered the body and turned into pus-filled sores that made the skin feel like it was on fire. If the eyes were infected, they became cloudy and eventually all sight was lost. And most of the victims were children. It was a sickness that terrified parents because they knew that one in every three children who got smallpox died, and those who lived were scarred or blind.

European doctors were helpless to stop the disease. They tried making pastes from plants and feeding patients herbal teas. They hung red curtains around the bed of the patient hoping that the color red might take away the sickness. They even tried having the patient chew dried horse manure. Nothing helped. The one thing they did know was that people who recovered from smallpox never got the disease again even if they nursed a person covered with smallpox sores. Once a person had smallpox, he or she was immune.

Doctors in the East were centuries ahead of European medicine. In 1000 CE, Chinese doctors had already discovered how to inoculate people against smallpox. They collected scabs from smallpox patients, ground them up, and blew the powder into the noses of healthy children. It was blown up the right nostril for a boy and up the left nostril for a girl. The child would become ill, but it was a much milder case of smallpox without the horrible scars and with little chance of death.

In India and the Arabic world, pus was collected from the sores of sick people. The physician then made a small cut in the skin of the healthy person and rubbed the pus into the slit. Within a few days, the person would be recovering from a mild case of smallpox and was immune for the rest of his life.

It wasn't until the 1700s that the British learned about inoculation. When Lord Montagu was named Ambassador to the Ottoman Empire, his wife attended a smallpox party in Constantinople. The amazed Lady Montagu wrote back to her friends that while she was at a party an old woman pulled from her skirts a nutshell filled with smallpox pus. The old woman asked who wanted the treatment and adults and children held out their arms. She scratched them with a sharp needle and rubbed the pus into the wound.

Lady Montagu told her friends that the people suffered a mild form of the pox and were not scarred for life. Lady Montagu had contracted smallpox when she was 26 and her face was horribly scared. She was convinced this was the way to spare her own children from scars and possible death. In 1717, she had her 6-year-old son take the treatment. It was successful and when she returned to England she had well-known surgeon Charles Maitland inoculate her 3-year-old daughter.

News of this new procedure spread quickly and soon surgeons throughout the British Empire were busy inoculating patients and experimenting with ways to improve the technique. One such scientist was Edward Jenner who began experimenting with the milder illness cowpox in the 1790s.

He had observed that milkmaids who had suffered cowpox were also immune to smallpox. And he began using cowpox as an inoculation ingredient. His experiments were quite successful because the patients had an even lower death and illness rate. The public was frightened about using a virus that came from cows. Cartoonists published pictures showing people growing horns and hooves because they took the cowpox inoculation.

But Jenner's vaccine was so good at preventing illness that it was accepted by both the medical community and the general public. By 1814, more than 3 million people in Europe had been vaccinated against smallpox. By the 1820s, smallpox vaccines were given around the world and Edward Jenner was recognized as the hero who stopped smallpox.

VanTassel-Baska, J., & Stambaugh, T. (2015). *Jacob's Ladder Reading Comprehension Program: Nonfiction Grade 3*, pp 37–39. London: Routledge. Used with Permission.

Simple Questions for Beginning Discussion and Modeling
The following are examples of simple questions to ask in guiding an initial discussion about the text.

- Main Idea or Message: What is the main idea or message in this text? (The discovery of a smallpox vaccine resulted from previous discoveries.)
- Point of View: What facts are included? (The text provides facts about the symptoms, facts about medical approaches in China, the East, and Britain, etc. What points of view are not included? The article does not include potential disadvantages about vaccines.)
- Context/Audience/Purpose: What is the purpose of the article? (To explain the evolution of how the smallpox vaccine became available to the general public.) How should you interpret the text? (The text is informational but allows the reader to appreciate a world without smallpox.) What words do you need to know to understand the text? (circular depressions, vaccine, inoculation) What places should we locate on a map to help us understand the text? (China, India, Constantinople, Britain)
- Techniques/Structure: How is the article structured? (Somewhat chronological order. It starts out in medieval times, discusses European difficulties, then describes the approaches of doctors in the East 1000 CE. Then, the text describes approaches in the 1700s and final success

in the early 1800s. During each approach, a different type of solution is offered.) How does the author use emotion or story? (The use of words such as smallpox "pus" and description of people losing parts of their lips, ears, and tips of their noses elicit strong reactions from the reader.) What can you learn from the illustrations? (The illustration of the doctor and boy help us understand the benefits of smallpox vaccines; the needle conveys the overall solution to the problem of smallpox.)
- Supporting Details: What are the three most important supporting details of the text that help enhance the main idea? (Descriptions of the negative effects of smallpox, past attempts to give a small amount of smallpox to individuals, and building upon prior successes with cowpox to apply to smallpox vaccinations.)
- Implications: What are the implications of contagious diseases on our current society? (Diseases can destroy lives, change lifestyles, and also lead to innovation.)

Complex Questions for Discussion and Differentiation
The following are examples of complex questions.

- Context/Audience/Purpose + Supporting Details: Why do you think the author chose to discuss the cowpox vaccinations? How does this support the author's purpose? (Including this detail helps us understand criticisms associated with the vaccine before it became available to the general public.)
- Point of View + Techniques: How do the facts presented enhance our understanding of problem-solution within the text? (The author provides facts such as grinding up smallpox scabs to put into the noses of children as a way to show various approaches to solving the problem.)
- Technique + Context/Audience/Purpose: Why did the author include descriptive details about smallpox for the audience? (Perhaps it creates a shock value for the reader and helps the reader appreciate life without smallpox and regard Jenner as a hero.)

Older Student Example: Rhetorical Analysis Wheel (Intermediate and Middle/Early High School): "9/11 Address to the Nation" – President George W. Bush
Before applying an in-depth analysis, students first need to understand the text they are reading. It may be necessary to guide students through some basic comprehension questions or paraphrasing of sentences. After students have an initial understanding of the text, lead students through completion of the Rhetorical Analysis Wheel, first by asking simple questions about each element, then by asking complex questions (how one element contributes to, interacts with, or impacts another). See Figure 4.1 for an example of how elements of the wheel connect across elements.

Simple Questions for Beginning Discussion and Modeling
The following are examples of simple questions to ask when guiding an initial discussion about the text.

- Context/Purpose: What is the historical context? What is the purpose of the speech? (Bush presented this speech on the evening of September 11, 2001, through a television broadcast following the terrorist attacks. His purpose is to respond to the terrorist attacks of 9/11 and to encourage the people to go forward in defending freedom.)
- Message/Claim: What is Bush's main claim? (Although the U.S. has been attacked, the American people are resolved to stay strong.)

- Point of View/Assumptions: What is Bush's point of view and what are his assumptions? (As president, Bush is speaking from a point of view of protecting and defending the nation. He makes an assumption in making no distinction between terrorists and those who harbor them.)
- Logos: What are his main points that help his argument make sense? (He explains how terrorist attacks affected citizens' lives, explains why America is strong, explains policy points, and concludes to move forward and defend freedom. He uses logical reasoning by stating America has stood down enemies and will do so again.)
- Pathos: What emotions are evoked within the speech? (He evokes shock, pride, patriotism, and also comfort.)
- Ethos: Is Bush's argument credible and trustworthy? How do you know? (He explains how he implemented the government emergency response, introduces policy points, and uses pronouns "we" and "us" to build connection with the audience.)
- Techniques: What literary or rhetorical techniques are used throughout the speech? What words have strong negative connotations? (He uses imagery – pictures of the planes; parallelism – foundations . . . foundations; shatter steel . . . dent the steel; metaphor – brightest beacon; several contrasts – the worst of human nature/best of America; Psalm 23 biblical allusion; negative word connotations such as "evil, despicable acts of terror," "mass murder," "chaos and retreat.")
- Structure: How does he structure his argument? What do you notice about the structure of his paragraphs and sentences? In what ways do you see the use of compare/contrast? (He presents the problem and solution through policy points. His speech includes several short sentences. The speech is to the point without undue elaboration. Compare/Contrast – terrorist acts intended to frighten, but they have failed, etc.)
- What are the implications of this document? (The War on Terror)

Complex Questions for Discussion and Differentiation
The following are examples of complex questions.

- Techniques + Pathos: How does he use techniques to evoke emotion? (He uses imagery to evoke a sense of shock; metaphor of America as a beacon to evoke patriotism; biblical allusion to provide a sense of comfort.)
- Structure + Logos: How does the use of structure enhance the logic of his argument? (By opening the speech with clear examples of real individuals who have lost their lives, he establishes a problem that must be solved. The solution details specific policy points to address safety.)
- Structure + Purpose/Context: How does the short sentence structure relate to the context and his purpose? (The American people needed to know direct information regarding the events of the day and what was to come. The brief sentences get to the point to provide clarity amid the chaos of the day.)
- Purpose/Context + Implications + Pathos: What are the implications of the emotional appeals on the audience? (The patriotic feelings toward America are meant to evoke a sense of pride about America's resolve and unity toward the War on Terror to continue to defend freedom.)

After analyzing the text for rhetoric, students should be able to apply their reasoning to justify an evaluation.

- Evaluation: How effective is he in supporting his claim? Is there a balance of pathos, ethos, and logos appeals? Is the claim fully supported? (Sample response – Bush uses a balance of appeals to support the claim that although America has been attacked, the American people are resolved to stay strong. He provides adequate facts about policy points. He uses extensive pathos appeals to evoke emotion.)

Note: The Text Analysis Wheel – Primary is a simpler version for analyzing informational text. If students are not ready to apply logos, pathos, and ethos appeals to analyzing text, students can analyze how an author develops a central idea through points and evidence along with the other elements (structure, purpose, techniques, etc.).

Creating Complex and Differentiated Questions Using the Text Analysis and Rhetorical Analysis Wheels

The Text Analysis Wheel – Primary and Rhetorical Analysis Wheel provide a framework for thinking about how the elements interact to develop a main idea, central idea, or claim in an informational text, article, or speech. These analysis wheels can also be used as a tool to differentiate questions, tasks, and assignments. You can design tiered questions that are deliberately differentiated toward increased complexity. The wheel is used to create questions that could be assigned to various groups based on their level of understanding or as a way to increasingly add more rigorous discussions in the classroom.

As shown in Table 4.1, Level 1 questions focus on understanding single elements on the wheel. Level 2 questions focus on interactions between two different elements on the wheel, and Level 3 questions combine three elements or encourage divergent thinking by asking students to manipulate elements on the wheel and discuss alternatives. When possible, add specificity from the text into

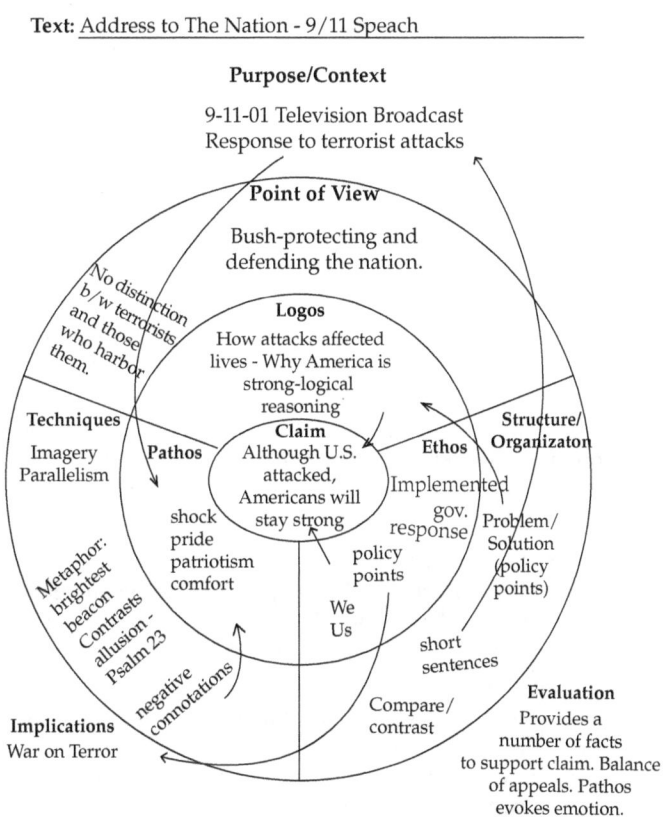

FIGURE 4.1 Example of completed Rhetorical Analysis Wheel – Bush's 9/11 Address to the Nation

the questions (e.g., how does the technique of repetition develop the tone and tone shifts throughout the speech?) as opposed simply asking a question using category names from the wheel (e.g., how do techniques influence the tone?).

Creating Complex and Differentiated Tasks

In addition to asking leveled questions, the following examples illustrate how the Text Analysis or Rhetorical Analysis Wheels can be used to create differentiated and complex tasks and activities. Begin by plotting where the typical assignment might fit on the wheel (i.e., which section or element does the grade-level task fit) and then add another element or interaction to the task. We provide several examples in Table 4.2 of grade-level tasks differentiated with complexity. Note that the task demands do not require students to discuss multiple and isolated elements of the wheel in succession but require

TABLE 4.1 Questions with increased levels of complexity: ELA informational texts

Increasing Levels of Complexity	Example Questions for "Pox on You"	Example Questions for "9/11 Address to the Nation"
Level 1: A single element	What bias do you notice in the text? Is the last statement in the text (Jenner is a hero) a fact or opinion?	What metaphors does Bush use throughout the speech? What words have strong negative connotations?
Level 2: Interaction of elements	Why is the chronological order in the text important? How does it support the message that Jenner was a hero?	What impact do his techniques (metaphor, negative connotations, etc.) have on pathos appeals?
Level 3: Manipulate elements and consider the possibilities or combine interactions among multiple elements	What if this were written for a younger audience? How would the headings, organization, and supporting details change?	Why is the sentence structure important for the context of the speech and what are the implications for the audience?

TABLE 4.2 Examples of differentiated complex tasks in ELA informational texts

Wheel	Grade-Level Task Example	Task Differentiated with Complexity Using the Wheel Elements
Use of Text Analysis Wheel – Primary	Create a letter to persuade others to participate in recycling. Include important details about the benefits of recycling.	Create a letter to persuade someone to participate in recycling. Include both facts and emotional appeals that will most be accepted by an audience of your choosing. Use the Text Analysis Wheel and interactions to plan your letter.
Use of Text Analysis Wheel – Primary	After reading ____, find the main idea and three supporting details. What is the structure of the text?	After reading ____, find the main idea and three supporting details. How are the ideas organized in a way that supports the author's purpose?
Use of Rhetorical Analysis Wheel	Create a blog entry from the perspective of an audience member who has just listened to President George W. Bush's speech. Discuss the techniques he used throughout the speech.	Create a blog entry from the perspective of an audience member who has just listened to President W. Bush's speech. Evaluate the effectiveness of his use of techniques on logos, ethos, and pathos appeals.
Use of Rhetorical Analysis Wheel	Develop a speech to persuade others on whether video games are harmful or helpful to young people. Use sufficient and relevant evidence to support your points.	Develop a speech to persuade others on whether video games are harmful or helpful to young people. Consider how your purpose influences the organization of your points and how specific techniques will evoke emotion within your audience.

students to think about the *interactions* between and among the elements. Essentially you are differentiating the criteria of the task demand by asking students to examine more complex relationships that support a richer understanding of a text.

Depending on student readiness, adding complexity to tasks or questions may not be enough of a challenge. Many of the current Common Core State Standards (CCSS) ELA standards already incorporate complexity with criteria for students to determine how elements contribute to other elements. Consider adding additional differentiation features such as depth and/or abstractness to tasks, assignments, or products as displayed in Table 4.5.

Depth

As with fiction and poetry, applying depth to ELA informational text analyses can be accomplished by asking carefully designed debatable questions. These questions may come in the form of "should" or "forced-choice" questions that require students to form an opinion with supporting evidence, justify a stance, conduct additional research to craft a response, or examine various possibilities, perspectives and scenarios. In ELA, evidential support is derived from the texts they read and the inferences they are making about those texts. Once the question is designed, students form an educated opinion or position based on the evidence and data (e.g., fiction or nonfiction texts and other resources available). Depth questions are not intended to be judgment-based queries that lack textual or other evidential support but larger, real-world questions that encourage students to form an opinion by interpreting textual evidence and making conclusions based on their own research or analysis.

An example of a depth question for the story, "Pox on You" could be "Should people try out new options before they are fully tested?" This question encourages students to examine the text, make inferences, and form an opinion that is justifiable from the text based on their individual interpretation or research. Similarly, for the speech, "9/11 Address to the Nation," the debatable (forced-choice) question "Is Bush effective in subduing fears?" allows students to use evidence from the text (and evidence from the Rhetorical Analysis Wheel) to justify their argument. Depth questions are useful especially for facilitating Socratic seminars, providing an overarching question for research, or guiding students to think through the question from multiple points of view.

Depth questions prompt students to engage with content deeply in order to sufficiently support their response. In exploring the depth question, students think as experts and figure out what they know and don't know to answer the question. Students can use elements of the wheel as a way to uncover content that would substantiate an argument. For example, students consider, "What do I know about this element (e.g., techniques)? How does this support or refute my argument?" For example, while answering "Is Bush successful in subduing fears?" from the "9/11 Address to the Nation," they consider how the elements and interactions of logos, ethos, pathos, and context support "yes, he is successful" or "no, he is not." Students may also want to conduct brief research on the historical event to understand the context of the speech to further justify their arguments.

Overarching Depth Questions

Debatable questions can be posed that would require multiple lessons, texts, or resources throughout a larger unit of study. In order to answer the question, students explore multiple points of view from various texts or media. For example, an overarching question for a unit might be, "Is war necessary for peace?" or "Does technology hurt or harm social relationships?" You can purposefully select resources that reflect a number of perspectives on the issue. Students answer the question by forming an opinion and providing evidence for their ideas and individual interpretations. Table 4.3 shows examples of how multiple resources can be used to explore the question "Is war necessary for peace?" from multiple perspectives. After examining this question through multiple texts, students write an opinion piece that incorporates examples from the four selected texts and their own research. This adds complexity through the examination of interactions between various elements and interactions between different text selections (i.e., different perspectives).

Depth Applied to Standards and Tasks

Questions that promote depth can be applied across all reading genres and disciplines. Debatable questions support the integration of multiple standards. When integrating standards with a depth question, combine a reading standard with a writing or speaking and listening standard. The writing or speaking and listening standards dictate the product selection while the reading standard provides guidelines for answering the questioning using the specific criteria required in a standard. The combination of multiple standards into one larger task also promotes complexity. As emphasized in Chapter 2, standards may also be accelerated for advanced learners as well as the readings and resources. Table 4.4 shows a few examples of how depth can be incorporated with several ELA standards and task demands related to informational texts.

TABLE 4.3 Overarching depth question for unit

Is war necessary for peace?			
"A Day of Infamy" – Franklin D. Roosevelt	*"Beyond Vietnam" –1967 – Martin Luther King, Jr.*	*Nobel Peace Prize Acceptance Speech – Barrack Obama (December 11, 2009)*	*"9/11 Address to the Nation-" – George Bush*
Yes – as a way to defend the United States.	No – argues for removal of troops from Vietnam because war is not leading to peace.	Argues for "just wars" only.	Yes – when in response to terrorism to defend freedom.
Write an argumentative essay that answers the question, "Is war necessary for peace?" Incorporate examples from at least three different articles or speeches we have read in class as well as your own research. Be sure to provide specific textual examples to support your argument.			

TABLE 4.4 Depth applied to standards and tasks in ELA informational texts

Question	*Product or Activity and Standard*	*Reading Standard*	*Specific Task Demand*
Should everyone be required to get flu shots?	Research Synthesis CCSS.ELA-LITERACY.W.2.7 Participate in shared research and writing projects (e.g., read a number of books on a single topic to produce a report; record science observations).	CCSS.ELA-LITERACY.W.2.8 Recall information from experiences or gather information from provided sources to answer a question.	Students use the question to guide on-going gathering of information, using multiple sources and media to examine different points of view on the issue.
Should robot dogs replace real dogs?	Perspectives Debate CCSS.ELA-LITERACY.SL.5.1.A Come to discussions prepared, having read or studied required material; explicitly draw on that preparation and other information known about the topic to explore ideas under discussion.	CCSS.ELA-LITERACY.RI.5.2 Determine two or more main ideas of a text and explain how they are supported by key details; summarize the text.	Students debate the issue from different stakeholder perspectives (parent, child, elderly in nursing home, animal shelter owner, tech industry).

Question	Product or Activity and Standard	Reading Standard	Specific Task Demand
Should schools require virtual learning on snow days?	Research Multiple Points of View CCSS.ELA-LITERACY.W.8.7 Conduct short research projects to answer a question (including a self-generated question), drawing on several sources and generating additional related, focused questions that allow for multiple avenues of exploration.	CCSS.ELA-LITERACY.RI.8.9 Analyze a case in which two or more texts provide conflicting information on the same topic and identify where the texts disagree on matters of fact or interpretation.	Students examine the question from specific points of view (teachers, parents, students, school board), noting the assumptions of each perspective. Students may read short articles related to the topic. This can be synthesized into a conclusion or proposal for the school community.
Should sports stars be paid less money?	Quick Debate CCSS.ELA-LITERACY.SL.9–10.1 Initiate and participate effectively in a range of collaborative discussions (one-on-one, in groups, and teacher-led) with diverse partners on grades 9–10 topics, texts, and issues, building on others' ideas and expressing their own clearly and persuasively.	CCSS.ELA-LITERACY.RI.9–10.6 Determine an author's point of view or purpose in a text and analyze how an author uses rhetoric to advance that point of view or purpose.	As part of a pre-reading activity, students stand on opposite sides of the room to defend their point of view. Then, when students read a specific text, they note the interactions among author's use of rhetoric, point of view, and assumptions toward the question.

Abstractness

Concept Map and Organizers

Abstractness is the connection of facts to broader ideas such as generalizations, rules, theories, concepts, laws, or principles. The incorporation of abstractness in ELA informational texts can be achieved in a variety of ways. You can introduce specific generalizations to students and ask them to connect ideas from a text to those generalizations, as indicated in Figure 4.2. A more detailed explanation and examples of generalizations is found in Chapter 2. Concept maps (see Chapter 2) are another effective tool for encouraging students to organize their ideas and amass facts into broader categories and specific generalizations. In this way students are not just discussing concepts on a general level but supporting specific generalizations with evidence from a variety of sources.

Table 4.5 shows an example of adding abstractness to the text "Pox on You." Students complete the concept organizer explaining how the text supports various generalizations about encounters. Students can continue to add to this handout as it applies to other stories or texts.

Another approach to incorporating abstractness is to provide a list of concept words that relate to the text. For example, from "Pox on You," the word list might be *discovery, innovation, conflict, change, power, influence, risk,* etc. This concept list serves as a word bank in which students create a sentence using at least two of these words that capture a major idea from the text. Students may write "Taking risks can lead to discoveries" or "Encounters of ideas lead to innovation" to convey a big idea that generalizes beyond the text.

Abstractness and the Big Idea Reflection

The Big Idea Reflection (see Appendix C2) is a way for students to think about concepts within a text, how those concepts relate to each other, and how those concepts apply to students' lives. This framework allows the students to consider the major ideas about the human experience that are captured within a text and then consider how these concepts relate to broad generalizations, issues in the current world, and students themselves. This is especially important to the discipline of language arts. Literature and many informational texts communicate ideas about life: problems, celebrations, successes, failures, accompanying emotions, and relevant culture. The Big Idea Reflection helps students recognize these ideas in a way that integrates the content with the learner.

Students may need guidance in understanding what is meant by an abstract concept. It may be useful to explain that these concepts are ideas that cannot be seen, heard, or touched. Provide student with examples such as change, power, order, structure, freedom, sacrifice, hope, etc.

Figure 4.3 shows an example of student responses for the Big Idea Reflection applied to "(9/11 Address to the Nation."

Generalizations for Adding Abstractness	*Textual Evidence from "Pox on You"*
Encounters cause conflicts and challenges.	The encounter with cowpox as a vaccine led the public to be frightened about being inoculated.
Encounters may require cooperation and teamwork.	People encountered news of using smallpox pus as a treatment. This news spread from Lady Montagu to her friends and eventually to surgeons who cooperated to improve the technique.
Encounters may lead to opportunities and threats.	The encounters with new knowledge (e.g., use of smallpox pus) led to other new knowledge (experimenting with cowpox).
Connection to another concept Encounters + _____	Encounters + change. Individuals encountered news which spread change to the medical community and the general public.

FIGURE 4.2 Concept Organizer: "Pox on You"

What	**Concepts** What concepts/ideas are in the text?	Power, resolve, freedom, change, terror, justice, unity, heroes
	Generalizations What broad statement can you make about one or more of these concepts? Make it generalizable beyond the text.	Freedom is protected by unity.
	Issue What is the main issue, problem, or conflict?	Terrorist attacks of 9-11. Thousands have died.
So What	**Insight on Life** What insight on life is provided from this text?	Even when the nation saw the worst of human nature, it saw the best of America through everyday heroes.
	World-Community-Individual How does this text relate to you, your community, or your world? What question does the author want you to ask yourself?	World- Terrorism is still a major threat to our world. The author wants me to consider "Am I willing to stand united to defend freedom?"
Now What	**Implications** How should you respond to the ideas in the text? What action should you take? What are the implications of the text? What can you do with this information?	The text makes me reflect about the everyday heroes who helped in the ways they did. Heroes come from tragedies. This information makes me wonder more about those who lost their lives and how their loved ones may feel. I want to learn how their memories are honored.

FIGURE 4.3 Big Idea Reflection – example "9/11 Address to the Nation" by George W. Bush

Checking for Understanding

If we teach in a way that encourages higher level thinking and expert thinking, then the tasks and activities that we ask students to complete need to mirror the instruction. Otherwise, how will we be sure that students understand the information presented? So, the tasks, products, and activities are also differentiated by applying depth, complexity, or abstractness in ways that mimic the instructional tasks and daily activities.

You can provide a more rigorous task for students by incorporating more than one differentiation feature. As noted in Table 4.5, the grade-level tasks are differentiated by including depth and complexity, complexity and abstractness, or abstractness and depth. This combination allows students to practice multiple applications of expert thinking within the task. Consider a student's readiness and pace of learning when determining the extent to which differentiation features are applied. Some standards may already include complexity by requiring students to consider how elements interact. In these instances, it is important that the resources or texts are above-grade level, or that above-grade level standards are used to plan instruction.

TABLE 4.5 Differentiated and advanced tasks with differentiation features: ELA informational text examples

Grade-Level Task	Differentiated and Advanced Task	Applicable Features of Differentiation
Develop an advertisement persuading people to get their flu shot. Use important facts and details to convey your message.	Develop an advertisement persuading people to get their flu shot. Intentionally use emotion/story, facts, and experience/expertise to persuade a specific audience (children, the elderly, etc.). Embed the idea of "encounters may lead to opportunities and threats" within your ad.	Complexity is added through the interaction of text elements (from the Text Analysis Wheel – Primary). Abstractness is added through the connection to "encounters."
Create an editorial that explains your point of view about the federal government's role in space exploration. Include important relevant examples to support your claim.	Create an editorial that explains your point of view about the federal government's role in space exploration. In your response, defend or refute the idea that "progress leads to more progress" with relevant examples. Enhance the credibility of your claim by addressing counterclaims and providing substantive research evidence.	Abstractness is added through the connection to "progress. "Complexity is added by including the interaction of rhetorical elements (from Rhetorical Analysis Wheel).
Read the article and answer the who, what, when, where, why and how questions related to the article content (i.e., main idea, author claims, evidence).	Should the government increase sales tax on sodas? Write an argumentative essay to justify your position with sufficient and relevant evidence from the assigned article and an article you found through your own research to support your points of view. Plan your argument using the Rhetorical Analysis Wheel, specifically structuring your argument with a counterclaim to enhance ethos and logos appeals. Use the article we read in class support for or against your idea.	Depth is added by incorporating a specific forced-choice question that allows the student to examine multiple perspectives of the issue (including the counterclaim and additional evidence) Complexity is added through the interaction of rhetorical elements (from the Rhetorical Analysis Wheel).
Create a Word Collage (using Wordle or other software) to show the most important phrases used throughout Bush's 9/11 speech. Include a description of how these words support his main claim.	Does tragedy lead to heroism? Choose words and phrases from Bush's 9/11 speech that support your point of view to create a Word Collage (Wordle or other software). Include a description of how these words support the idea "freedom requires sacrifice."	Depth is added by incorporating a forced-choice question that must be justified with evidence from the text. Abstractness is added by asking students to support a generalization about freedom.

Conclusion

The informational text models serve as tools for students to analyze how an author develops a main idea, central idea, or claim through the purposeful craft of language, structure, and techniques. This framework builds a content base for learning about communication through rhetoric and provides a structure for recognizing the ways in which authors develop strong claims. Such skills are especially important for students to discern so that they can critically reason through the information that is presented to them. In this way students grow to be critical consumers of knowledge and thoughtful contributors to the world rather than passive in-takers of information.

5

Models for Differentiating Instruction in Social Studies

Shakespeare's quote "What is past is prologue" captures the core question of historical thinking – how did events in the past shape the present? Social studies is the interconnected study of social sciences (NCSS, 2013). This includes the study of how history, economics, politics, geography, and other factors influence the way people lived in the past, and how the interaction of these factors affects the present and future.

Using the models to be described, we can guide students to understand that history and social studies are not just about learning disconnected facts, rather, they are about understanding the complexities of cause-effect within a larger system (Winkler et al., 2016). The frameworks can also support issue-analysis where students explore problems in history and discern the value of other solution options. For example, students might examine how alternative decisions to a given issue would have affected multiple social, political, economic, or cultural factors. Students can also develop the skills needed for analyzing primary source documents through applying interpretations of local, global, past, present, and future perspectives, evaluating and corroborating sources for credibility, and challenging assumptions.

In this chapter, we provide examples of how to use models for examining ideas, events, and people in history in ways that guide cause-effect analysis. We provide examples of how differentiation features of complexity, depth, and abstractness can be applied to questioning, tasks, and products within social studies so that students have opportunities to think deeply in ways that promote the habits of an expert and encourage them to internalize processes inherent to the field.

Instructional Ideas and Models for Adding Complexity in Social Studies

Adding complexity to instruction in social studies promotes students' understanding of cause-effect relationships by providing an explicit framework for how different social studies factors (e.g., geography, economics, culture, etc.) interact. The Social Studies Connections Wheel (see Appendix A7) is useful when teaching students about a time period, civilization, era, person, historical idea, or event. Beyond students learning about the basic sequence of events in history, the Social Studies Connections Wheel promotes students' thinking about the complexities of cause-effect within a larger system of subsystems. Using this model, students not only identify causes and effects, but they also learn to analyze the long-term impact of history through a broad comprehension of the context. Additionally, they learn to construct and evaluate the strength of historical arguments for why things happened as they did.

To bridge students to thinking like a historian, students need to learn critical analysis skills to evaluate bias, credibility, point of view, and a document's intended impact on an audience. These process skills can be taught through the use of the Primary Source Analysis Wheel (see Appendix A8). Using this model, students analyze a primary source document by applying critical analysis to the features and ideas within the text. The wheel can serve as a tool for inquiry in which students can challenge assumptions within a text and interpret multiple sources to support a historical argument with evidence. The Primary Analysis Wheel provides a model for the explicit reasoning expert historians use to examine problems and ideas within historical contexts.

Both the Social Studies Connections Wheel and the Primary Source Analysis Wheel may be used with a variety of age and readiness levels. The analysis wheels support instruction for the teacher and the learner. For example, you can use the model as a planning guide for differentiating instruction and lesson planning or explicitly teach the model to students as a way to analyze social studies content or a primary document and internalize expert thinking and inquiry. The specific instructional strategies used depends upon the purpose, classroom context, student readiness level, learning pace, and exposure to the wheel.

Using the Social Studies Connections Wheel

To begin using the Social Studies Connections Wheel, it is necessary for students to have background information on the topic, idea, event, or person. It may be used throughout a unit of study for students to revisit and make new connections over time. It is important to note that unlike the Literary Analysis Wheel and the Text Analysis Wheel, the Social Studies Connections Wheel may take multiple weeks to complete as students gain more background knowledge and add to various sections of the wheel before being able to make specific connections. Once students have acquired some basic information about the historical event or idea, you can guide students through each factor (What were the economic conditions? What do we know about the culture? About the social structure?) and then ask complex questions about how the factors relate (e.g., How did the geography affect the economy?).

Questions can be differentiated from simple to complex by combining multiple factors of the wheel in ways that ultimately guide students toward an in-depth understanding of the cause-effect relationships between the factors. It is important to help students see the connections visually by drawing arrows among multiple factors of the wheel to indicate relationships. It is not necessary to explicitly teach all components of the wheel, and some factors may not be relevant to the given historical situation.

Overall, the use of the Social Studies Connections Wheel allows students to see a more integrated view of a historical situation. The framework provides a structure for thinking about multiple cause-effect relationships and how they interact as a system. In the following section, we provide examples of using the Social Studies Connections Wheel for younger grades (Pilgrims traveling to Plymouth) and intermediate/middle school students (Renaissance starting in Italian city-states).

Example 1: Social Studies Connections Wheel – Pilgrims Travel to Plymouth

After students have an initial understanding of content about the Pilgrims traveling to Plymouth (through video, class discussion, readings, etc.) lead student through completion of the Social Studies Connections Wheel, first by asking simple questions about each factor, then by asking complex questions (how one element contributes to, interacts with, or impacts another).

Simple Questions for Beginning Discussion and Modeling
The following are examples of simple questions to ask in guiding an initial discussion.

- Context/Era: What is the context? Early 17th Century Europe and early America (1620 and years prior)
- Geography: Where did the Pilgrims live? Where did they move to? (They first lived in England, then they moved to the Netherlands, then to Plymouth, New England.)
- Economics: What do we know about the economic situation? (Many Pilgrims could not find work in the Netherlands. They worked with the Adventure Merchanters of London to finance the trip to Plymouth.)
- Culture: What do we know about the culture and religion of the Pilgrims? (They were Separatists, a Puritan group that separated from the Anglican Church of England. They were still influenced by medieval culture – seasonal festivals and folklore. As Separatists, they were Protestant Puritans that wanted to purify the Anglican Church. They thought it had too much power over its church members. They did not sing hymns or celebrate Christmas or Easter. Many were called "traitors" for separating from the Church of England and some were imprisoned.)
- Conflict: What conflicts relate to the Pilgrims? (They were persecuted for their beliefs by the Church of England; the Church and State were one).
- Politics/Government: What role did the government play? (The Church of England and the King of England were unified. Their rules infringed on the beliefs of the Separatists. The Separatists wanted to "purify" the Church of England from its worldly practices.)
- Social Structure: What do we know about the social structure (family, education, etc.)? (Separatists were outcasts of the English society. If they did not attend services in the Anglican Church in England, they had to pay a fine. In the Netherlands, they did not fit in with the culture. It was difficult to understand the Dutch language and find work, so they were also somewhat outcasts.)
- Innovation: What new technologies or scientific discoveries influenced the Pilgrims? (The invention of the printing press and distribution of the Bible influenced the Protestant Reformation – which influenced Puritan beliefs about the interpretation of the Bible.)
- World Context: What else was happening in the world during this time? (Other colonization throughout the world; Thirty Years' War involves tension between England and Spain, causing concern for the trip to America and settling in Virginia.)

Complex Questions for Discussion and Differentiation
The following are examples of complex questions.

- Economics + Geography: How did the economic situation in the Netherlands impact the Pilgrims' decisions to move to Plymouth? (As there were not any opportunities to obtain jobs in the Netherlands, Separatists did not want to stay, so they sought a new settlement.)
- Culture + Politics/Government: How did the Church of England's power influence the culture of the Separatists? (Though they were persecuted, the Separatists did not change their faith, they sought to practice their faith elsewhere. When they moved, they felt the Netherlands' culture was destructive to their children. They felt they were losing their English identity.)
- Culture + Conflict: Why did their religious beliefs lead to conflict? (Their interpretation of the Bible and response to the political power of the Church caused their conflict with the Church of England.)

Example 2: Social Studies Connections Wheel: Why did the Renaissance begin in Italy?
In this example, students examine the question, "Why did the Renaissance begin in Italy?" By examining multiple sources over time, students determine how various factors on the wheel interact to cause change. See Figure 5.1 for an example of the completed Social Studies Connections Wheel related to the Renaissance.

Simple Questions for Beginning Discussion and Modeling
The following are examples of simple questions to ask in guiding an initial discussion about the Renaissance.

- Context/Era: What is the context? 1350–1600 – Europe (especially Italy during early Renaissance)
- Geography: What is unique about the geography of Italy? (Italy's geography is surrounded by the Ligurian, Tyrrhenian, Mediterranean, Ionic, and Adriatic Seas, allowing the spreading of ideas through trade routes.)
- Economics: What was the economic situation during the time of the Renaissance? (Some individuals were wealthy because of the finances inherited from family members who died during the Black Plague. The economy was based on money instead of bartering, which increased a need for banking. Wealthy merchant families such as the Medici families could sponsor artists. City-states became places for the manufacturing of goods, which brought profit.)
- Culture: What do we know about the culture of Italy during this time? (Though they were still Christian in their faith, they were influenced more by humanism – the idea of valuing the creation, writing, and thinking of humans more than the revering of God/religion.)
- Conflict: What conflicts or problems influenced the Renaissance? (Because of the invasion of the Turks, many Byzantine scholars moved to Italy, and they brought with them ideas and artifacts of the ancient world. *Fewer* conflicts and invasions increased order over time, allowing for stability. The plague may be considered a "conflict" as it caused widespread disease just prior to the Renaissance.)
- Politics/Government: What role did the government play? (The Church and State were one, but there was not a centralized source of power. Merchant families such as the Medici had power. Italian city-states could hire strong armies, increasing stability within the city-states. They collected taxes, which helped develop infrastructure.)
- Social Structure: What do we know about the social structure (family, education, etc.)? (Unlike other parts of Europe, they did not have a feudal system where peasants paid to stay on nobles' land through the production of crops. After the Black Plague, there was a shortage of workers, and the peasants could begin to demand payment for their labor, causing people to move to cities.)
- Innovation: What new technologies or scientific discoveries happened during the Renaissance? (They rediscovered the works of ancient scholars such as Plato – from the Byzantine scholars. Also, they rediscovered Latin and old scientific writings. This inspired developments in math and also understanding the universe – the sun as the center. DaVinci is known for his inventions and great art flourished because artists were sponsored by patrons.)
- World Context: What else was happening in the world during this time? (Columbus landed in the Americas; expansion of Indian trade routes; people continued to be influenced by Marco Polo's writings and artifacts brought from Asia.)

Models for Differentiating Instruction in Social Studies ◆ 51

Text: Renaissance

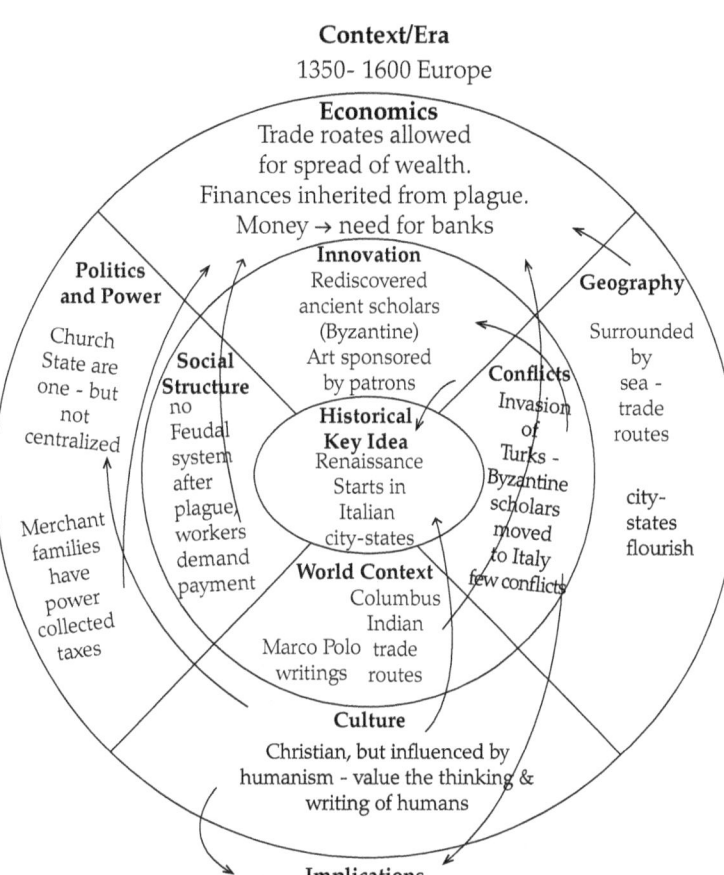

FIGURE 5.1 Example of completed Social Studies Connections Wheel – Renaissance

Complex Questions for Discussion and Differentiation

The following are examples of complex questions.

- Geography + Economics: How did geography influence economics and how did this influence the "rebirth" of ideas? (The Italian city-states controlled some of the trading routes. The Medici family of merchants developed banking systems to control long-distance trade. The wealthy could spend their money on patronizing artists. In addition, worldly scholars were attracted to move to Italy, thus continuing the spreading of new ideas.)
- Innovation + Conflict: How did conflicts influence new ideas in the Renaissance? (The *absence* of conflict allowed for political and economic stability, which allowed individuals to be concerned with issues beyond survival – the arts. The recent invasion of the Turks in the Ottoman Empire caused the Byzantine scholars to move to Italy, where they brought the ancient works of the Greeks, which inspired innovation in math, science, philosophy, etc.)
- Economics + Politics and Power: How did the political power influence the economic growth during the Renaissance? (The Italian city-states were able to charge taxes, which influenced better infrastructure. They were able to hire armies and bureaucrats to run the cities which produced stability.)

Using the Primary Source Analysis Wheel

To begin using the Primary Source Analysis Wheel, it is necessary for students to have background information on the context of the time period. Therefore, they should apply the knowledge they learn through a unit of study as they explore the content of a document, artifact, poster, political cartoon, or photograph.

First, it is helpful to establish a purpose for looking at the document. For example:

- Why are we learning about this?
- Are we trying to develop a historical argument for why an event occurred?
- Are we trying to understand more about a problem for this particular time period and place?
- Are we seeking to understand more about the way of life during this context?
- Are we exploring multiple points of view about an issue in order to provide an interpretation of history through various lenses?

The purpose for looking at the document will set the stage for how evidence within the document is examined. Most of the inner wheel can be answered by looking closely at the source itself. This may be the easiest place for students to start by answering – Who wrote this? When? What details do I notice? What is the issue here? What are the main ideas and points? The outer wheel involves the process skills that historians use to interpret texts (examining the context, impact over time, use of sourcing, evaluating bias, challenging assumptions).

Some of the analysis may require background knowledge or additional research using sources to compare and contrast against the document. The outer wheel itself could serve as a Know, Want to Know, Learned (KWL) chart – What do we know about the context and what do we need to know? How could we find this information out? Mirroring the thinking of an expert in the field, the tool provides a framework for continued inquiry, guiding students to consider what they do and do not know from the evidence provided.

Questions can be differentiated from simple to complex by combining multiple factors of the wheel in ways that ultimately guide students toward an in-depth understanding of the interaction between the concepts. It is important to help students see the connections visually by drawing arrows between multiple elements of the wheel to indicate relationships. It is not necessary to explicitly lead students through all the components of the wheel, and some factors may not be relevant to the given historical situation or document.

Overall, the use of the Primary Source Analysis Wheel allows students to think as a historian by applying critical analysis, credible sourcing, and historical comprehension of context to the interpretation of primary sources. In the following section, we provide examples of using the Primary Source Analysis Wheel to a visual poster about sugar rationing in World War I and to a speech by President Obama.

Example of Primary Source Analysis: "Your Sugar Ration is 2 lbs. per month" (c. 1918) – U.S. Food Administration

In this example, students critically examine the primary source: "Your Sugar Ration is 2 lbs. per month" (c. 1918) – U.S. Food Administration as noted in Figure 5.2.

Before applying an in-depth analysis, students first need to have a context for what they are viewing. It may be necessary to provide background information about rationing during war time, particularly during World War I. After students have an initial understanding of the context, lead students through completion of the Primary Source Analysis Wheel, first by asking simple questions about

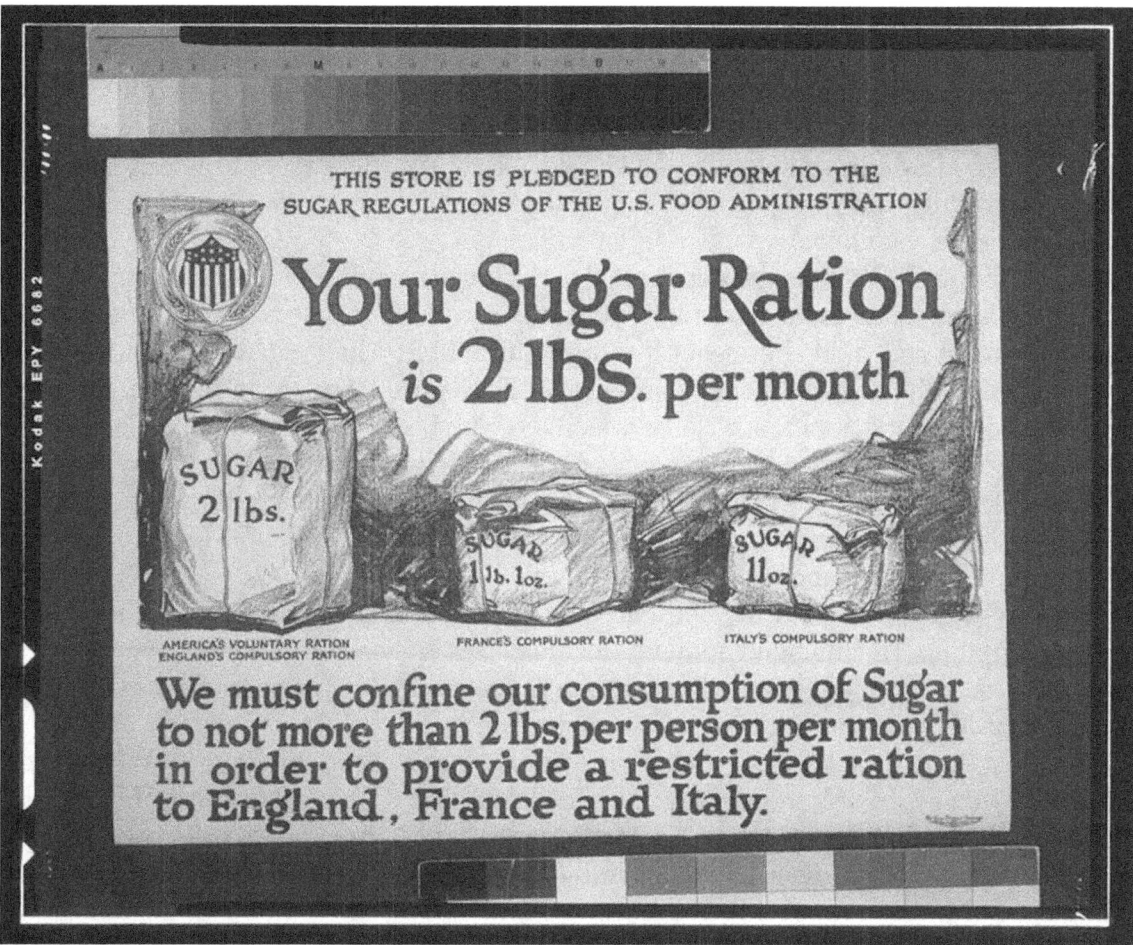

FIGURE 5.2 Primary source: "Your Sugar Ration is 2 lbs. per month"

each element, then by asking complex questions (how one element contributes to, interacts with, or impacts another). For an example of how elements of the wheel connect across elements.

Simple Questions for Beginning Discussion and Modeling

The following are examples of simple questions to ask in guiding an initial discussion about the primary source.

- Purpose (Author's Purpose and Learner's Purpose): What is the author's purpose in creating this? (To show support for the U.S. regulations on sugar rations.) What is my goal as I study this source? (To seek to understand the document's meaning within the context of the time.) Note: the learner's purpose will vary depending on the lesson purpose established by the teacher.
- Point of View: What is the author's point of view? What assumptions are made? Are biases present? What were others' points of view about this source? What is my point of view? How can this be viewed from an economic perspective? Political perspective? Geographic perspective? (There is an assumption that some Americans could be unhappy about the 2 lb. sugar ration. From an economic perspective, the message implies the conservation of goods can help support the war. From a geographic perspective, this shows insight into how the U.S. ration affects the rations of other countries. This document shows a loyalty to the U.S. political perspective of following the voluntary ration.)

- Context: When and where was this written? What else was happening during this time? (global, local, prior to and after?) (This poster was made around 1918 and put in U.S. grocery stores. Farms in Europe were made into battlefields and many farmers in Europe and the U.S. went to war, leading to a decrease in crop production. Ships crossing the Atlantic were also threatened. The U.S. Food Administration was developed, led by President Woodrow Wilson, to help conserve, distribute, and transport food for the war effort. In World War II, rations were also used to support the war effort.)
- Impact/Influence: What is the impact of this document over time? on the current day? On the future? (Posters such as this caused the consumption of meat, wheat, fat, and sugar to decrease by 15 percent and food shipments to Europe to double. The food was sent to soldiers who needed strength on the battlefields in Europe. They were also sent to Europeans, many malnourished from a lack of food. Herbert Hoover, who became a future president, developed a voluntary program, drawing on citizen's compassion and patriotism for the war effort. After World War I, Hoover continued to organize efforts to transport food to those starving in central Europe. Similar rationing practices were made in World War II. People learned canning practices to conserve food and used special recipes.)
- Author/Audience: Who is the author? Who is the intended audience? (United States Food Administration. The intended audience includes U.S. citizen store visitors.)
- Issue: What is the main issue or problem in the document? (The war effort needs to be supported through citizens' sacrifice – rationing sugar.)
- Main idea/Concepts: What are the main points being made in this source? What concepts or ideas do you see in this source? (In order for other allies to have sugar, it is important to voluntarily buy only 2 lbs. of sugar. England, France, and Italy have a set "compulsory" ration. A major concept is sacrifice. Overall, abiding by the ration will help the war effort so that soldiers and allies in Europe will have food.)
- Credibility: How reliable is this source? How do you know? Can we trust the source? Does the language used match the time period? (The document is from the U.S. Food Administration. The top left symbol adds credibility to its message. A student-historian may consider comparing this to other posters from the U.S. Food Administration during this time as they relate to food rations.)
- Organization/Techniques: How are the information/images organized? Why? What specific techniques are used? (The use of comparison is intentional to show how much more sugar U.S. citizens have as their voluntary ration. The emblem in the top left corner provides credibility to the document.)
- Evidence: What details do I notice? What other evidence do I need? What other corroborating evidence is needed? What inferences can I make from this evidence? What questions do I need to ask? (Students may take note of the word "voluntary" for the U.S. ration. The word "pledged" conveys a sense of patriotism and loyalty to the cause. Students may want to ask additional questions and look at other posters from this time period in order to further gain insight into their purpose of looking at the document – to seek to understand its meaning within the context of the time.)

Complex Questions for Discussion and Differentiation

The following are examples of complex questions.

- Issue + Impact + Evidence: What was the impact of sugar rationing on the war effort? What evidence do you need to answer this question? (Students may explore other documents and research sources to answer this question.)

- Point of View/Perspective + Organization/Techniques: What does the author assume of the audience and how do we know this from the techniques used? (The author may assume that the customer may not think the 2 lb. ration is enough. The visual comparison allows the viewer to see how much more sugar they have as a "voluntary" ration compared to the other countries.)
- Context + Audience: How did the context of World War I and sugar rationing affect the "audience" customer? (The audience may have been compelled to abide by the sugar ration out of a sense of patriotism or compassion for the other countries. Conservative cooking practices and reduced sugar recipes were used. Note: other outside sources are needed to answer this question.)

At the end of the analysis, students may have new questions they want to explore. You might ask, "What do we still want to know about the impact of this document? How could we find that out?" Remember, the wheel itself can serve as a type of KWL Chart, prompting students to consider more about the purpose of the U.S. Food Administration and more about the impact of sugar rationing in the U.S. and other parts of the world.

Example of Primary Source Document: President Obama's Speech at Kennedy Space Center April 15, 2010

In this example, students examine "President Obama's Speech at Kennedy Space Center April 15, 2010" (accessible online) with the Primary Source Analysis Wheel. Before applying an in-depth analysis, students first need to understand the text they are reading. You may choose to show a video recording of the speech. It may be necessary to guide students through some basic comprehension questions or paraphrasing of sections. After students have an initial understanding of the text, lead students through completion of the Primary Source Analysis Wheel, first by asking simple questions about each element, then by asking complex questions (how one element contributes to, interacts with, or impacts another).

Simple Questions for Beginning Discussion and Modeling

The following are examples of simple questions to ask in guiding an initial discussion about the primary source.

- Purpose (Author's Purpose and Learner's Purpose): What is the author's purpose in writing this? (President Obama wants to inform the audience at Kennedy Space Center how he will continue to support a revitalized National Aeronautics and Space Administration (NASA).) What is my goal as I study this source? (To seek to understand Obama's stance on space funding.) Note: the learner's purpose will vary depending on the lesson purpose established by the teacher. Teachers may ask students to read a text to justify a point of view, etc.
- Point of View: What is the author's point of view? What assumptions are made? Are biases present? What were others' points of view about this source? What is my point of view? How can this be viewed from an economic perspective? Political perspective? Geographic perspective? (Obama believes NASA is accomplishing good things, but some of the programs need to be revitalized. He believes NASA should not pursue going to the moon again. Efforts should focus on deep space exploration. His assumption is that space exploration is not a luxury, but an essential part of the quest for a brighter future. Some view the collaboration with private companies and other countries as a threat to the U.S. leadership in space. Some express concern over spending money on solving problems in space rather than solving problems on the ground. Others, including Buzz Aldrin, disagreed with cutting the Constellation program. Obama points out a number of economic benefits for jobs in the space travel industry, especially in Florida.)

- Impact/Influence: What is the impact of this document over time? On the current day? On the future? (This speech and the initiatives it describe pave the way for new research and technology for deep space exploration. Future implications include building a heavy-lift rocket, sending astronauts to an asteroid, and eventually sending humans to orbit and land on Mars.)
- Context: When and where was this written? What else was happening during this time? (global, local, prior to and after?) (This speech was delivered April 15, 2010, at the Kennedy Space Center. Obama speaks of the effects of a recession on the U.S. budget, but actually increases funding to NASA by $6 billion. The space shuttle program was nearing its scheduled retirement, causing some to worry about their own future and the future of the space program.)
- Author/Audience: Who is the author? Who is the intended audience? (President Obama presents the speech at the Kennedy Space Center; much of the content is focused on NASA and its leadership, though the general audience includes Americans. Some in NASA were concerned about changes including the cutting of programs and new strategies to work with private businesses and other countries.)
- Issue: What is the main issue or problem in the document? (Increasing NASA's budget. Space exploration is worth it because it helps lives on Earth. NASA's budget has decreased or increased depending on political winds.)
- Main idea/Concepts: What are the main points being made in this source? What concepts or ideas do you see in this source? (There is a plan to study space beyond Earth's low orbit, space exploration will create jobs, and the space program improves lives and society. Major concepts include discovery, innovation, research, investment, environment, and efficiency.)
- Credibility: How reliable is this source? How do you know? Can we trust the source? Does the language used match the time period? (The text can be checked against the video recording. Obama builds credibility in his speech by recognizing former astronauts, senators, and congressmen and women who have supported NASA. Obama's language reflects 21st Century dialect in referring to individuals by their first name, referring to individuals as "folks" and stating phrases such as "I thought that was very cool.")
- Organization/Techniques: How are the information/images organized? Why? What specific techniques are used? (He ends with the broad benefits of space exploration for humanity, leaving the audience with a sense of inspiration. He repeatedly uses "we will" and "our goal" to include himself as part of NASA, building connections with the audience. He uses parallelism near the end – "greatest achievement in NASA history . . . human history" – to evoke emotion and connection. He uses contrast - "beginning of something or the end of something" – to inspire the audience.)
- Evidence: What details do I notice? What other evidence do I need? What other corroborating evidence is needed? What inferences can I make from this evidence? What questions do I need to ask? (Obama cites a number of benefits to deep space exploration from past to future benefits. Past: improvements for health and well-being; satellite navigation, water purification, aerospace manufacturing, medical imaging, Tang, personal inspiration; future: increased Earth-observations to improve understanding of climate; getting into space more affordably, probe to the Sun's atmosphere, a new advanced telescope, and future inspiration.)

Complex Questions for Discussion and Differentiation
The following are examples of complex questions.

- Organization/Techniques + Point of View: How does the author's point of view affect the way the document is organized? How does the use of specific techniques reveal bias or the author's assumptions? (Obama begins the speech by recognizing the legendary astronauts who have accomplished NASA's past goals. This builds credibility as he discusses parts of NASA that are ending – space shuttle program and Constellation - and builds a case for how he supports new goals for NASA. He says "I am 100 percent committed to the mission of NASA and its future" to rid the audience of doubt about his new strategy to rely on private businesses and other countries.)

- Main idea/Concepts + Author/Audience: Why might the author choose these particular concepts and ideas for the given audience? (Because the audience is committed to NASA's mission, Obama presents the ideas of innovation and discovery into deep space as part of America's continued quest, not just an afterthought. Obama justifies the increased funding and cutting of some programs by emphasizing increased job opportunities and benefits for life on Earth.)

Creating Complex and Differentiated Questions for Social Studies

The Social Studies Connections Wheel provides a framework for thinking about how various factors such as economics, geography, or culture influence one another regarding a particular historical event. The Primary Source Analysis Wheel allows students to critically interpret the interactions of ideas, various elements of a text, and the source's context. These wheels can also be used as a tool to differentiate questions, tasks, and assignments. You can design tiered questions that are deliberately differentiated toward increased complexity. The wheel is used to create questions that could be assigned to various groups based on their level of understanding or as a way to increasingly add more rigorous discussions in the classroom.

As shown in Table 5.1, Level 1 questions focus on understanding single elements on the wheel. Level 2 questions focus on the interaction between two different elements on the wheel, and Level 3 questions combine three elements or encourage divergent thinking by asking students to manipulate elements on the wheel and discuss alternatives. When possible, add specificity from the historical context in the questions (e.g., How does the geography of New England influence the political boundaries of the colonies?) instead of just asking a question using category names from the wheel (e.g., How does geography affect politics?).

Creating Complex and Differentiated Tasks for Social Studies

The following examples further illustrate how the Social Studies Connection Wheel can be used to create differentiated assignments. Simply plotting where the typical assignment might fit on the wheel (i.e., economics, geography, conflict, etc.) and then adding another factor or interaction to the task requirement creates a more complex task. We provide several examples in Table 5.2 of grade-level tasks differentiated

TABLE 5.1 Questions with increased levels of complexity: Social Studies

Increasing Levels of Complexity	Example Questions for lesson – Pilgrims traveling to Plymouth	Example Questions for Primary Source – "Your Sugar Ration is 2 lbs. per month"
Level 1: A single element	What was the main conflict for the Pilgrims while in Europe?	What is the main message about rationing within the document? What assumptions does the creator make about American citizens?
Level 2: Interaction of elements	How did the political power of the Church of England influence the culture of the Separatists?	What can we infer about the store owner's purpose from the details in the document?
Level 3: Manipulate elements and consider the possibilities or combine interactions between multiple elements	What would have happened if the Pilgrims had stayed in the Netherlands? How would this have impacted their everyday life and economic situation?	How do the techniques used by the creator provide insight about economic, geographic, and political perspectives within the context of 1918?

TABLE 5.2 Examples of differentiated complex tasks: Social Studies

Analysis Wheel	Typical Assignment	Differentiated with Complexity Using the Wheel Elements
Social Studies Connections Wheel	Draw a map of Mesopotamia. Describe where you would want to live and why.	Draw a map of Mesopotamia. Explain how the geography influenced trade and the development of power in the area.
Social Studies Connections Wheel	Make a timeline for the major events of the Civil War. Choose three events and explain their significance.	Make a timeline for the major events of the Civil War. What would have happened if the Battle of Gettysburg had not taken place? What effect would that have had on future events? Use the factors from the Social Studies Connections Wheel to explain your response.
Social Studies Connections Wheel	Make a list of all the factors that contributed to the Fall of Rome. Categorize these causes. Imagine you are in the role of leadership 10 years before the Fall of Rome. Identify at least three areas of vulnerabilities and create a plan for how you would address them.	Imagine you are in a leadership role ten years before the Fall of Rome. Identify at least three areas of vulnerability and create a plan for how you would address them by discussing how various factors on the Social Studies Connections Wheel influence each other (e.g., stronger economics may produce more political stability).
Social Studies Connections Wheel	From the perspective of someone living in the Renaissance, write a first-person account about the exciting times of the Renaissance! Explain how the new ideas of the Renaissance are affecting your daily life.	From the perspective of someone living in the Renaissance, write a first-person account about the exciting times of the Renaissance! Explain how the Renaissance is making an impact on daily living by referring to the ways multiple factors (e.g., culture, social structure, politics, economics, innovation, etc.) influence change.
Primary Source Analysis Wheel	Analyze the primary source document using a graphic organizer to answer: What details do you notice? What is the point of view? What new questions do you have?	Analyze the primary source document using the Primary Source Analysis Wheel. How does the creator's use of techniques and organization reveal assumptions or bias in the document?
Primary Source Analysis Wheel	If you were an individual living during the time period studied, how would you respond to the ideas in the primary source document? Write a journal perspective explaining your thoughts on how those ideas influence your thinking.	If you were an individual living during the time period studied, how would you respond to the ideas in the primary source document? Write a journal perspective explaining how you interpret the problem (within the document) through your local point of view and how the main ideas in the document might influence your daily life.
Primary Source Analysis Wheel	Analyze the primary source document, then explain how its message would affect different groups of people.	Analyze the primary source document, then explain how its concepts and main ideas had an impact over time in local and global contexts.

with complexity. Note that the task demands do not require students to discuss multiple and isolated elements of the wheel in succession but require students to think about the *interactions* between and among the elements.

Other Applications of the Social Studies Wheels

The Social Studies Connections Wheel and Primary Source Analysis Wheel can be used in a number of ways in the classroom to foster thinking as an expert. Beyond analyzing the causes and effects of historical events and ideas, students can apply a historical issues-analysis to evaluate decisions and actions. *The Public History Initiative of UCLA* (UCLA History, 2021) describes the skills of historical issues-analysis as the following:

> the ability to identify problems that people confronted in historical literature, the local community, and the state; to analyze the various interests and points of view of people caught up in these situations; to evaluate alternative proposals for dealing with the problem(s); and to analyze whether the decisions reached or the actions taken were good ones and why.

In examining the actual historical solutions to a given problem (e.g., war, laws, treaties, innovation), using the Social Studies wheels, students can apply a historical issues-analysis by exploring alternative solution proposals to a given problem in history. They might examine how these alternatives would have produced different effects on various factors on the wheel. In other words, in answering "what if" questions (e.g., "What if the events of 9/11 had not occurred on American soil?") students examine how decisions have multiple implications on society.

The Social Studies Connections Wheel allows students to explore the multiple factors that should be considered to determine the extent to which decisions and actions were justified and why. While examining alternative proposals, they can follow the effects of such proposals by examining the long-term implications on the economy, culture, social structure, etc.

The following are other examples of how the Social Studies wheels can be used during a unit, study, lesson, problem-solving applications, and integration with ELA.

- ◆ Over the course of a unit, you may ask students to add notes to a bulletin-board sized Social Studies Connections Wheel, adding relevant information over time to aspects of the wheel. As lesson content is introduced, you can ask complex questions to help students make connections between the factors.
- ◆ Use parts of the wheel as a way to facilitate jigsaw activities. One group of students may focus on politics and power, another group on social structure, and another group on innovation (for a given society, era, or event), etc. After initial research and learning, students from the various groups can come together and make connections between the different social studies factors.
- ◆ Students can use the Social Studies Connections Wheel to think through real-world current global issues in social studies. For example, students participating in Model United Nations may use the wheel to map out how a problem such as the lack of education for girls (in Third World countries) must be understood in the context of a nation's economy, government, social structure, and culture. Students may examine the impact of girls' schooling on multiple factors of the wheel to understand how developing a mock resolution to solve a problem will also have multiple effects on society.
- ◆ The wheels can be applied to problem-based learning as a way to engage students in exploring social or historical problems within social studies. During the problem identification stage, the Social Studies Connections Wheel can be a way for students to understand how various factors caused a problem to happen. For example, the interaction of trade (economics) within the Italian city states (geography) before the Renaissance created a context for spreading the bubonic plague.
- ◆ Students can examine real-world current issues such as "Should students be required to wear school uniforms?" using the Social Studies Connections Wheel. Students can examine the cultural influences, policies, family dynamics, education contexts, and other possible influences to answer the question. Other examples of current event issues include "What is the impact of social media on current society and the future?" or "Why are obesity rates higher in some states more than others?" By thinking about the multiple influences and

implications of the issue, students can understand the broader context of the issue within an interactive system of factors.
◆ Students can examine how various factors of the wheel come together to create solutions. For example, "The Mayflower Compact" is a result of new ideas developed because of the religious conflicts in Europe (conflict) and the opportunity for a new government (politics and power) in a new colony (geography).
◆ As students study famous individuals in history, they can apply the Social Studies Connections Wheel to research how the factors (geography, culture, social structure) impacted on the person's life while also showing how the person affected various aspects on the wheel.
◆ Complexity can be added to timelines by asking students to show the short and long-term implications of the event on various aspects of the wheel.

Depth

Applying depth to social studies content can be accomplished by asking carefully designed should or forced-choice questions that require students to form an opinion with supporting evidence, justify a stance, conduct additional research to craft a response, or examine various possibilities, perspectives, and scenarios. Such questions allow students to develop a substantial historical argument. In social studies, evidential support is derived from the content students learn during instruction, texts they read (including primary source documents), and the inferences they make about those texts. Once the question is designed, students form an educated opinion or position based on the evidence and data (i.e., primary and secondary sources and other resources available). Depth questions are not intended to be judgment-based queries that lack evidential support but larger, real-world questions that encourage students to form an opinion by interpreting evidence and making conclusions based on their own research or analysis. Depth questions should also be based on evidence that meets a standard, purpose, or goal and also considers the context of the district. Some debatable questions taken out of context could quickly become divisive or offensive. Consider the questions or problems and documents historians might use to solve a problem. Know your context and ensure you are using appropriate and approved primary sources and questions for debate. Depth questions are especially useful for facilitating Socratic seminars, providing an overarching question for research, or guiding students to think through the question from multiple points of view.

For a lesson about the Pilgrims traveling to Plymouth, the question "Should the Pilgrims leave the Netherlands to travel to Plymouth?" encourages students to examine the content presented (through text, video, class discussion), make inferences, and form an opinion that is justifiable from the content. Similarly, for a lesson about the Renaissance, the debatable question "Could the Renaissance have happened within a feudal system?" allows students to use evidence from various sources and consider the multiple factors of influence (from the Social Studies Connections Wheel) to justify their argument.

These depth questions can also be applied within the context of studying a primary source document. For example, in analyzing Obama's speech at the Kennedy Space Center, the question "Should the federal government fund space initiatives?" can be examined using the Primary Source Analysis Wheel as a guide to think through various perspectives (past, present, and author's perspective), context (local, global), and NASA's influence over time. As students study the U.S. sugar rationing document, they may explore the piece from the perspective of a U.S. citizen in 1918 with the question "Should we willingly ration our sugar?" Students can answer the question by examining how details address assumptions and perspectives about rationing for the audience of the time.

Depth questions prompt students to engage with content deeply in order to support their response adequately. In exploring the depth question, students think as experts and figure out what they know and don't know to answer the question. Students can use elements of the wheel as a way to uncover content that would substantiate a historical argument. For example, students consider, "What do I know about this element (e.g., politics/power)? How does this impact other factors and how does this support or refute my argument?" For example, while answering "Should the Pilgrims go to Plymouth?" students use the thinking skills of a historian to consider how the elements of the economic, political, and cultural situation interact to support or refute their decision. Students may also want to conduct additional research to justify their arguments.

Overarching Depth Questions

Debatable questions can be posed that require multiple lessons, texts, or resources throughout a unit of study. In order to answer the debatable question, students explore multiple points of view from various resources. For example, an overarching question for a unit on Westward Expansion might be, "Was the American West a land of opportunity?" Students answer the question by forming an opinion and providing evidence for their ideas and individual interpretations. Table 5.3 shows examples of texts that might be used to explore this question from multiple perspectives. After examining this question in multiple texts and perspectives, students write an opinion piece that incorporates examples from the three selected texts and their own research.

Depth Applied to Standards and Tasks

Questions that promote depth are applied across multiple texts and disciplines. Debatable questions support the integration of multiple standards. When integrating standards with a depth question, social studies standards can be combined with an ELA writing or speaking and listening standard. The writing and speaking and listening standards serve the basis for the product selection while the social studies standard provides guidelines for answering the question using the specific criteria required in a standard. The combination of multiple standards into one larger task also promotes complexity. Standards may also be accelerated for advanced learners. Table 5.4 shows several examples of how depth can be incorporated with several social studies standards and task demands.

Other debatable questions that relate to other social studies content may include:

- Is fair trade "fair" to both parties?
- Is globalization harmful or helpful for Third World countries?
- Does the Constitution give too much power to the federal government?
- Should taxes be increased to support a government-sponsored mission to Mars?
- Who was more "magnificent" – Mehmed II or Suleiman the Magnificent?
- Was Ancient Greece a true democracy?

TABLE 5.3 Overarching depth question for social studies unit

Was the American West a land of opportunity?		
Cherokee Perspective	Pioneer Perspective	Art
"Our Hearts are Sickened" by John Ross (1836)	Catherine Haun, "A Woman's Trip Across the Plains in 1849" journal entries	American Progress, John Gast (1872)

Write an opinion piece that answers the question, "Was the West a land of opportunity?" Incorporate examples from at least three different primary sources we have examined as a class as well as your own research. Be sure to provide specific textual examples to support your opinion.

62 ◆ Models for Differentiating Instruction in Social Studies

TABLE 5.4 Depth applied to standards and tasks in social studies

Question	Product or Activity and Standard	Social Studies Standard	Specific Task Demand
Would you rather live in an urban or rural community?	Quick Debate CCSS.ELA-LITERACY.SL.1.1.B Build on others' talk in conversations by responding to their comments through multiple exchanges.	(Tennessee: 1.1- Grade 1) Explain with supporting details the culture of a specific place, including a student's community and state.	At the introduction of a unit on community, students stand on opposites of the room to defend whether they prefer to live in an urban or rural community. The question can be revisited as students learn more content about each type of community and how this way of life is affected by various factors on the Social Studies Connections Wheel.
Should the Pilgrims leave Europe to settle in Plymouth?	Choice-Reasoning Chart – Humanities CCSS.ELA-LITERACY.SL.3.1 Engage effectively in a range of collaborative discussions (one-on-one, in groups, and teacher-led) with diverse partners on grade 3 topics and texts, building on others' ideas and expressing their own clearly.	(Massachusetts: 3.3- Grade 3) Identify who the Pilgrims were and explain why they left Europe to seek religious freedom; describe their journey and their early years in Plymouth.	Students discuss the issue by thinking through the reason for making the decision, the evidence to support each decision, and the implications of each decision (see Figure 5.3)
Should we (colonists) join the Loyalists or the Patriots?	Class Debate and Written Response CCSS.ELA-LITERACY.W.5.1 Write opinion pieces on topics or texts, supporting a point of view with reasons and information.	(Florida: SS.5.A.5.7- Grade 5) Explain the economic, military, and political factors which led to the end of the Revolutionary War.	Prepare for a debate to the question, Should we (colonists) join the Loyalists or the Patriots? Use evidence from multiple primary sources to support a written opinion piece following the debate.
Should the government have the right to eminent domain?	4-Corner Debate (for pre-writing) CCSS.ELA-LITERACY.W.5.1.B Provide logically ordered reasons that are supported by facts and details.	(Tennessee: 5.50- Grade 5) Use specific textual evidence from primary and secondary sources to summarize the success, failures, and challenges of President Roosevelt's New Deal policies.	After reading various documents, students will take the perspective of a landowner, government, citizen of the community during the New Deal, and current present-day citizen. In a short written piece, students will answer the question from a given point of view, using evidence from various sources.

Models for Differentiating Instruction in Social Studies ◆ 63

Question	Standard	Activity
Would it be better to live in ancient Athens or ancient Sparta?	Discuss the issue from various perspectives (women, child, military, citizen) CCSS.ELA-LITERACY.SL.6.1.A Come to discussions prepared, having read or studied required material; explicitly draw on that preparation by referring to evidence on the topic, text, or issue to probe and reflect on the ideas under discussion.	(Florida: SS.6.W.3.3- Grade 6) Compare life in Athens and Sparta (government and the status of citizens, women and children, foreigners, helots).	Using a graphic organizer, students work in groups to discuss the question through various perspectives (woman, child, military, citizen).
Did the Industrial Revolution lead to progress or destruction?	Visual Continuum CCSS.ELA-LITERACY.W.8.8 Gather relevant information from multiple print and digital sources, using search terms effectively; assess the credibility and accuracy of each source; and quote or paraphrase the data and conclusions of others while avoiding plagiarism and following a standard format for citation.	(Massachusetts: WHII.6- Grade 8) Summarize the social and economic impact of the Industrial Revolution.	As a research gathering activity, students write evidence to support ideas along a visual continuum (e.g., a line drawn on a piece of paper or bulletin board) placing their evidence where it fits along the continuum for supporting progress or destruction. If done as a group, evidence can be written on sticky notes along a visual continuum.

Should or Debatable Question Should we leave Europe to go to Plymouth?			
Stakeholder or Character's Purpose or Goal To have a better life.			
Choice 1 Stay in the Netherlands		Choice 2 Go to Plymouth	
Assumption The situation will not change in the Netherlands.		Assumption If we leave the Netherlands, we will be able to maintain our culture and religious beliefs without persecution.	
Evidence/Inference Difficult to get a job. Difficult to raise children in the Netherlands. Children are not going to be raised as "English." Difficult to assimilate within the culture (hard to understand language).		Evidence/Inference Jamestown was a successful colony. We have an opportunity to go with a financial sponsor.	
Positive Implications (short and long-term)	Negative Implications (short and long-term)	Positive Implications (short and long-term)	Negative Implications (short and long-term)
We have a safe place to live free of persecution.	Children may grow up with a Dutch way of life. We lose a sense of our English identity. Difficult to be employed.	We could start a new way of life, freedom to worship, and freedom to maintain our cultural identity.	We would have to endure a long trip. We would risk death through disease and/or starvation if agriculture fails.
What other criteria, questions, or information should be considered to achieve the purpose or goal? How safe is the trip? Who will go? What do we know about the successes and failures of Jamestown?			

FIGURE 5.3 Choice-Reasoning Chart – Humanities example
Source: Adapted from "Reasoning about a Situation or Event" by Center for Gifted Education, n.d., retrieved from http://education.wm.edu/centers/cfge/curriculum/teachingmodels. Copyright 2015 by William & Mary, Center of Gifted Education.

Depth: Choice-Reasoning Chart

The Choice-Reasoning Chart – Humanities (see Appendix B1) provides a structure for students to apply elements of critical thinking (Paul & Elder, 2019) as they make decisions about debatable questions. As students reason through a question, they first think through their purpose. From here, various choices can be considered. Beyond thinking through each choice, students can examine underlying assumptions (e.g., values and beliefs), the evidence and inferences considered with each choice, along with the positive and negative implications of each choice. This structure allows students to make more sophisticated judgments in constructing arguments, going beyond simply justifying choices with evidence. Figure 5.3 shows an example of the Choice-Reasoning Chart – Humanities applied to Plymouth.

Abstractness

Concept Maps and Organizers

Abstractness is the connection of facts to broader ideas such as generalizations, rules, theories, concepts, laws, or principles. The incorporation of abstractness in social studies can be achieved in a variety of ways. You can introduce specific generalizations to students and ask them to connect ideas from a lesson or text to those generalizations, as indicated in Figure 5.4. A more detailed explanation and examples of generalizations is found in Chapter 2. Concept maps (see Chapter 2) are another

Generalizations for Adding Abstractness	Relating Content to Renaissance
Structure promotes function or malfunction.	Because of the strong economy, the armies could be paid and function well, allowing for the flourishing of ideas within a stable society.
Structure and function create cause-effect relationships.	The structure of the geography of the Italian city-states made Mediterranean trade possible, which produced economic stability and the spreading of foreign ideas.
Parts of structures interact to help achieve a purpose.	The wealthy nobility (part of the structure of society) had money to sponsor arts and sciences. Many foreign artists moved to Italy for this reason, bringing in new ideas.
Connection to another concept Structure + _____	Structure + Progress The political and economic structures of the Renaissance gave rise to innovation which enabled Western civilization to make considerable progress in the arts and sciences over time.

FIGURE 5.4 Concept Organizer – the Renaissance

effective tool for encouraging students to organize their ideas and amass facts into broader categories and specific generalizations. In this way students are not just discussing concepts on a general level but supporting specific generalizations with evidence from a variety of sources.

Figure 5.4 shows an example of adding abstractness to studying ideas about the Renaissance. Students complete the concept organizer explaining how the ideas of the era support different generalizations about the concept of structure. Students can continue to add to this handout as it applies to other lessons.

Another approach for incorporating abstractness is to provide a list of concept words that relate to the historical idea, event, or situation being studied. For example, after lessons on the Renaissance, the word list might include *innovation, science, change, progress, rebirth, power*, etc. This concept list serves as a word bank from which students create a sentence using at least two of these words that capture major ideas relating to the Renaissance. Students may write "The decentralization of power brought progressive innovation to civilization" to convey a generalization about the Renaissance.

Checking for Understanding

If we teach in a way that encourages higher level thinking and expert thinking, then the tasks and activities that we ask students to complete need to mirror the instruction. Otherwise, how will we be sure that students understand the information presented? So, the tasks, products, and activities are also differentiated by applying depth, complexity, or abstractness in ways that mimic the instructional tasks and daily activities.

You can provide a more rigorous task for students by incorporating more than one differentiation feature. As noted in Table 5.5, the grade-level tasks are differentiated by including depth and complexity, complexity and abstractness, or abstractness and depth. This combination allows students to practice multiple applications of expert thinking within the task. Consider a student's readiness and pace of learning when considering the extent to which differentiation features are applied. Some standards may already include complexity by requiring students to consider how factors within a historical situation interact. In these instances, it is important that the resources or texts are above-grade level, or that above-grade level standards are used to plan instruction.

TABLE 5.5 Differentiated and advanced tasks with differentiation features: social studies examples

Grade-Level Task	Differentiated and Advanced Task	Applicable Features of Differentiation
Complete a biography report about the life of William Bradford, the governor of Plymouth. Include information about his life before and after coming to Plymouth.	Complete a biography report about the life of William Bradford that describes his response to, "Should we leave Europe to travel to Plymouth?" In your report, include an explanation of how ideas about culture, conflict, geography, and money relate to one another.	Includes depth through the debatable should question from the perspective of William Bradford. Includes complexity by asking students to consider how various factors relate to one another.
Develop a visual to show and explain why the Renaissance started in the Italian city-states and not in other parts of Europe. Explain how the systems in the Italian city-states allowed an exchange of ideas more so than in other parts of Europe.	"Interactions may be positive, negative, or mutually beneficial." Develop a visual to show how interactions within the Italian city-states support this generalization. Explain how these interactions allowed changes in scientific innovation, culture, and social hierarchies and why these interactions would be less likely to happen in other parts of Europe.	Includes abstractness by incorporating the concept of "Interactions." Includes complexity by asking students to explain how multiple factors (from the Social Studies Connections Wheel) cause change.
Create a museum exhibit showcasing the life of Susan B. Anthony. Use information from primary and secondary sources to explain her significance today.	Create a museum exhibit around the idea "Individuality is an agent for change" to showcase the experiences of Susan B. Anthony. Was she a rebel or a hero? Use information from primary and secondary sources to answer this question from a present-day perspective and from the perspective of her time period.	Includes abstractness by incorporating "individuality" as a concept. Includes depth through the use of a forced-choice question that must be explored within multiple perspectives and contexts.
Write an editorial in response to the voluntary sugar rations during World War I in the U.S. Share your opinion on the extent to which it impacts the war.	Write an editorial in response to the voluntary sugar rations. Explain how the economic principle of rationing affects others in Europe and the conflict in World War I. Connect your explanation to the generalization "Parts of structures interact to help achieve a purpose."	Includes complexity by asking students to think about how multiple factors relate to one another (geography, economics, conflict). Includes abstractness by incorporating "structure" as a concept.

Conclusion

The models discussed in this chapter serve as tools that guide students to understand the complex cause-effect relationships between the social sciences and how accounts of the past must be critically interpreted within various contexts (a point of view, local, global, past, present, or future). These frameworks provide a foundation for students to build a historical comprehension of the role of people, ideas, and events and their long-term impact on society. Additionally, these models provide a structure for recognizing the relationships between the interconnected facts and details of history and current contexts so that students discern their value in shaping the present. Such skills are crucial for students as they think about how present civic decisions have multiple implications on creating the future.

Adding Differentiation Features through Social Studies Project Choices

The social studies project choices below showcase a variety of ways students can demonstrate their understanding of a lesson or unit topic. These ideas are popular projects that are often given to grade-level students, but here they are differentiated with complexity, depth, and/or abstractness in order to provide more challenge. Note that you will need to incorporate specific content within the assignments relevant to the social studies lesson or unit.

- Create a three-minute video documentary that shows the impact of _____ on at least two parts of the Social Studies Connections Wheel. Explain how the world would be different without _____. (Complexity)
- Develop a newspaper article for a specific event relating to _____. Explain how at least three social studies factors create cause-effect within your article. (Complexity)
- What important decision did individuals have to make at this time? Create a question that leads to two choices (Should we _____ or _____? Is it better to _____ or _____?) Complete the Choice-Reasoning Chart – Humanities to think through the issue, using evidence from your research to consider choices. (Depth)
- Develop a plan for a museum exhibit about _____ . What details are important to include to capture the attention of your audience? What medium will you use? (Short videos? Pictures with captions and explanations?) Use evidence from primary and secondary sources to show how your exhibit relates to the idea "Encounters lead to threats and opportunities." (Abstractness)
- Develop four questions to ask _____ in a mock interview. Within your questions, ask about cause-effect relationships that include factors on the Social Studies Connections Wheel. Provide answers from evidence in your research. (Complexity)
- Develop a pamphlet that teaches children about the importance of event, idea, person. Include the way in which at least three factors from the Social Studies Connections Wheel affected the event/idea/person and how the event/idea/person affected three factors. (Complexity)
- After conducting a biography study on _____, present information through a first-person account, explaining how all parts of the Social Studies Connections Wheel impacted your life. Then, explain how your life made a significant impact on at least two areas. (Complexity)

Created by Tamra Stambaugh & Emily Mofield, 2022

6

Models for Differentiating Instruction in STEM Fields

To move students toward expertise in science, it is important for them to have a strong foundation in a variety of interdisciplinary fields as science discoveries involve a combination of skills including the use of technology and mathematics. Scholars in STEM apply a set of interrelated skills to ask questions, solve problems, and explain phenomena in the world around them. Though most students may not conduct original STEM research until later in their academic career, they can be taught how to scientifically apply logic, analyze articles and findings, ask and test new questions, model ideas, and provide mathematical explanations.

Because of the interrelatedness of STEM skills and the emphasis on STEM education as a whole, we have constructed this chapter in a way that illustrates how the differentiation features of complexity, depth, and abstractness can be applied within and across different STEM areas. We selected examples that cut across multiple disciplines and scientific fields. The models shown can be applied to any STEM area, even if not represented here. We show examples of questioning, tasks, and products within STEM fields that encourage students to think deeply in ways that promote the habits of an expert and encourage them to internalize processes inherent to these interrelated and intra-related disciplines, particularly when engaging with the world around them, explaining new phenomena, and building upon previous knowledge to ask new questions and make new discoveries.

Instructional Ideas and Models for Adding Complexity in STEM

Adding complexity to STEM fields promotes students' understanding of how scientists, engineers, and mathematicians think. This thinking is supported through the STEM Analysis Wheel (see Appendix A9 and Figure 6.1). You will notice that the inner circle of the wheel includes the Next Generation Science Standards (NGSS) Cross-Cutting Concepts while the outside of the wheel lists the processes of thinking like a scientist, engineer, and mathematician, for example.

In this chapter, we provide examples of how STEM content may be approached through a variety of content and lenses using the wheel or the complexity features. The wheel model for adding complexity (see Figure 6.1) supports instruction for the teacher and the learner. You can use the model as a planning guide for differentiating instruction and lesson planning or explicitly teach the model to students as a way to help them analyze a scientific article, create a new experiment, or determine the implications of findings from their own investigations, thus modeling expert thinking and inquiry. We provide examples across multiple STEM fields to illustrate how the model may be used in a variety of situations and contexts. The model focuses on scientific/STEM thinking and cuts across multiple disciplines. As explained in Chapter 2, scientists vetted the wheel content based on their own field, whether that was engineering, geology, astronomy, biology, or medicine. While there are definitely nuances within each specific scientific field there are also similarities and guiding principles in how scientists

DOI: 10.4324/9781003238515-6

STEM ANALYSIS WHEEL GUIDE

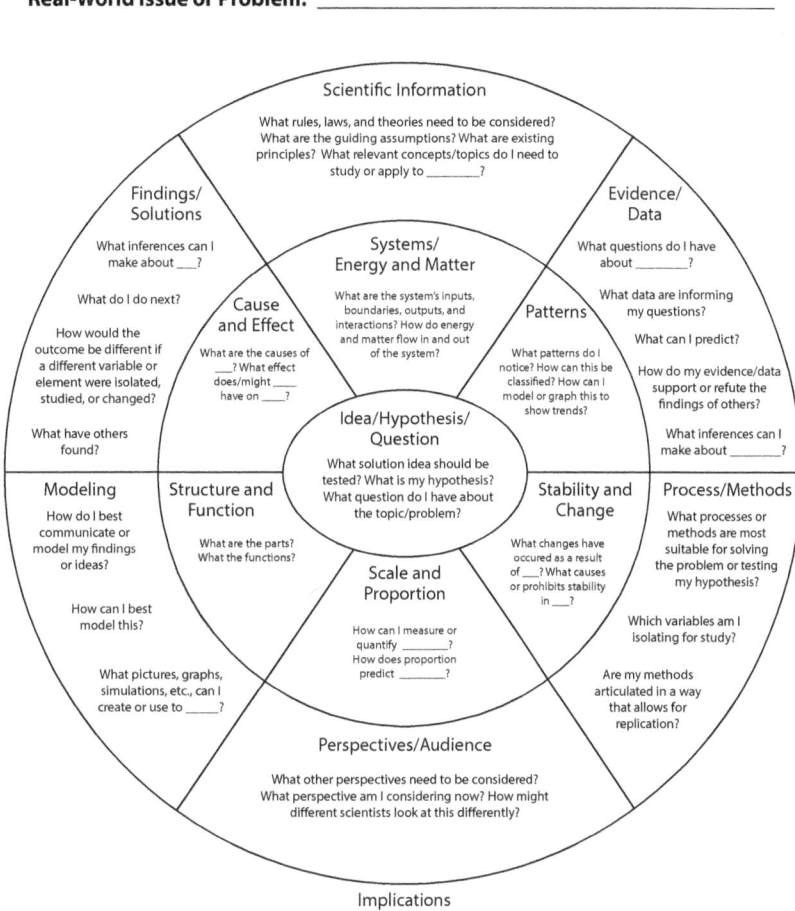

FIGURE 6.1 The annotated STEM Analysis Wheel

approach tasks. Of course, the specific instructional strategies used depend upon the content, instructional purpose, classroom context, student readiness levels, and prior exposure to this type of thinking and the actual model. Additionally, technology, for the purposes of our discussion, is viewed as a tool of the discipline. Most technology goals and standards in K-12 are clustered around the following: a proficient use of a variety of technological tools to further a goal, data organization, or communication of findings. Therefore, technology may best be incorporated across multiple disciplines as part of product creation or the tools of a given discipline.

Using the STEM Analysis Wheel to Differentiate Questions and Lead Discussions about Scientific Principles or Phenomenon

The STEM Analysis Wheel can be used in a variety of contexts for analyzing articles and determining next steps, thinking through a solution or design, analyzing a design, or planning an experiment, for example. Students may revisit the wheel multiple times throughout a unit as they come to different stages of investigating phenomenon or learning more. Consider the example shown in Figure 6.2 in which students watch a video to learn more about food webs and food chains. After students have watched the video,

Topic: Students watch a video on food webs and food chains prior to discussing the simple and complex questions.	
Simple Questions (single elements on the wheel to guide initial discussion)	*Complex Questions (interaction of two or more elements on the wheel or manipulation of elements to guide more complex discussions)*
What is the difference between a food web and a food chain? How might you model a food web in our community? Sketch your ideas and be prepared to explain your example. How is energy transferred in a typical food chain? What effect might population growth have on food webs and food chains? How would a food chain be affected if we had more predators than prey in an ecosystem?	Scale/Proportion + Modeling: How might you design a model that shows what would happen if one element of the food chain were eliminated? Be prepared to illustrate the effects. Cause and Effect + Scientific Information: What do we know about the effects of scarcity in food chains and how that impacts other animal and human systems? Perspective and Audience + Processes and Methods: How might an ecologist go about determining whether or not a food web would be impacted by the introduction of weed killer? Scientific Information + Systems/Energy/Matter: What do we know about food webs and food chains that would help us hypothesize what might happen to the food chain if there were significant weather changes (e.g., more cloudy than sunny days; significant changes in temperature)?

FIGURE 6.2 Simple and complex question examples using the STEM Analysis Wheel
Source: Adapted from Stambaugh et al. (2018), pp. 106–108. Prufrock Press. Used with permission.

Problem or Task: Design a footbridge for the local zoo that can cross a 5′ x 10′ chasm, is water resistant, holds up to 20 people safely, and is handicapped or stroller accessible.	
Simple Questions to Begin Thinking About the Design	*Complex Questions for Design Thinking*
Scientific Information: What information do I already know about creating bridges that will help me in my design? Findings/Solutions: What have other engineers done to solve this problem? What do other bridges look like? Modeling: What do I anticipate my final product will look like? How can I model it? Methods/Processes: How can I test my ideas? What methods will I use? Findings/Solutions: What solutions meet all of my criteria? Scale and Proportion: How can I model my ideas on a smaller scale before building? How will I know my ideas will work when built out on a larger scale?	Stability and Change + Processes/Methods: How can I test the stability of my design under weather and weight changes? Scientific Information + Findings/ Solutions: How do Newton's Laws inform the solutions I might come up with? Modeling + Audience: Does my model accurately test for possible collapse if too many students jump on it? Evidence/Data + Processes/Methods: What evidence and data can I collect to confirm that my methods for designing this structure are sound?

FIGURE 6.3 Differentiating questions in engineering using the STEM Analysis Wheel

you may use the wheel to differentiate questions, gradually increasing the complexity of the questions or assigning specific questions to different students based on their background knowledge, experience, and understanding of the content You can simply ask the questions as part of a discussion, or you can write different responses on the wheel and draw arrows to show interactions. Figure 6.2 outlines simple and complex question examples that may be asked using the wheel as a guide.

The STEM Analysis Wheel can also be used as a problem-solving and planning tool as students work through design thinking tasks such as engineering problems or experiments. Figure 6.3 shows an example of such planning. Students may begin by asking simple questions on the wheel and then move toward combining and considering multiple factors and interactions as their designs or experiments progress.

TABLE 6.1 Examples of differentiated questions using the STEM Analysis Wheel

Increasing Levels of Complexity	Example Questions for Discussing Cloud Seeding	Example Questions for Creating and Analyzing Graphs and Charts
Level 1: A single element	Scientific Information: What scientific evidence do we have to support cloud seeding? Cause and Effect: What effects does cloud seeding have on the environment? Structure and Function: Why are cumulus clouds targeted for cloud seeding? What is it about their structure that enables cloud seeding to happen?	Scientific Information: What information do you need to consider when creating a graph to show you findings? Processes and Methods: What is the best type of graph to communicate your findings?
Level 2: Interaction of elements	Scale and Proportion + Scientific Information: How often can cloud seeding be done without causing harm? What information or evidence suggests this, or do we need to collect?	Scale and Proportion + Cause and Effect: What effect does the scale of the graph have on the interpretation?
Level 3: Manipulate elements and consider the possibilities or combine interactions between multiple elements	Scale and Proportion + Cause and Effect + Modeling: What would happen if we increased the salt to water ratio. Would this necessarily produce more rain? Create a model to show the interactions and possible outcomes of various ratios. Make a recommendation.	Scale and Proportion + Cause and Effect + Modeling/Representation: What would happen if you increased the range of the numbers you want to display by 150? Would the scale and type of graph used change?

Additionally, you can design tiered questions that are deliberately differentiated toward increased complexity. Level 1 questions focus on understanding single elements on the wheel. Level 2 questions focus on interactions between two different elements on the wheel, and Level 3 questions combine three elements or encourage divergent thinking by asking students to manipulate elements on the wheel and discuss alternatives.

Table 6.1 gives two examples. The first example (second column) shows simple and complex questions for discussing cloud seeding. In this scenario students read an article about cloud seeding and discover that cloud seeding occurs when a salt and water solution is inserted into a cumulus cloud. The saltwater solution creates particles of ice that become heavy enough to fall from the cloud into the atmosphere and produce precipitation. The wheel is used to create questions that could be assigned to various groups based on their level of understanding or as a way to increasingly add more rigorous discussions in the classroom and a complex understanding of the phenomenon to the lesson. The third column shows a similar example with mathematics and the creation of graphs and charts.

Integrating Complexity in Mathematics and Technology

Mathematics is an important part of scientific investigation and integral to understanding scientific phenomena and calculating and interpreting results. Math is needed for modeling, determining scale and proportion, communicating results, providing evidence, articulating patterns, applying measurement, explaining precise processes and methods, and interpreting information and findings. All of these components are embedded within the STEM Analysis Wheel. Similarly, the use of technology is important to science as technology allows scientists and researchers to simulate scenarios through models, better communicate findings, or use specialized and computerized instruments. Students may be asked to apply mathematical principles in the following ways to add complexity to tasks:

◆ Examine the relationship between two different graphs
◆ Determine how to best display data based on different scales

- Identify patterns in different processes and methods or findings and solutions
- Show the probability of a specific event occurring at random or a predicted rate
- Provide precise measurements (decimals, fractions, scale and proportion)
- Create or program computer-based models to solve a problem or simulate data
- Design or apply equations that show cause and effect relationships
- Apply logic and proof to scientific information presented or gathered.

You can also find mathematical connections linked to the NGSS.

Depending on student readiness, adding complexity to tasks or questions may not be enough of a challenge. Many of the current NGSS standards already incorporate complexity with criteria for students to determine how elements interact within systems – especially as students acquire additional knowledge. Consider adding additional differentiation features such as depth and/or abstractness to tasks, assignments, or products as displayed in Table 6.5.

Depth

Applying depth to STEM can be accomplished by asking carefully designed debatable questions. These questions may come in the form of should or forced-choice and even "how do or how might I" questions that require students to form a hypothesis with supporting evidence, justify an idea or results from an experiment, conduct additional investigations to craft a response, or model ideas and scenarios. In STEM, evidential support is derived from the scientific information provided through articles and texts, scientific investigations or experiments, and the conclusions being drawn that inform new questions or next steps. Once the question is designed, students form an opinion or position based on the evidence and data. Depth questions are not intended to be judgment-based queries that lack textual or other evidential support nor are they to be ethically bound questions. Instead, depth questions are derived from real-world questions that encourage students to engage in scientific thinking and experimentation and draw conclusions based on their own research or analysis or a variety of scientific articles – especially those that include differing solutions or findings. Therefore, it is important to expose students to multiple studies or ideas and solutions that investigate similar problems in different ways. In STEM, to determine depth questions it is helpful to begin by asking ourselves what problems a practicing professional in the field might encounter, ask, or solve. Of course, we also want students to ask their own questions and solve their own problems. Some students may be ready to ask their own depth questions based upon their own curiosity and investigations. Table 6.2 shows some examples of depth questions that may be answered or investigated in STEM categories.

Depth questions prompt students to engage with content deeply in order to sufficiently support their response. In exploring the depth question, students think as experts and figure out what they know and don't know so that they can gather appropriate information to answer the question. Students can use elements of the wheel as a way to uncover content that would create a new idea, experiment, or analyze previous information accumulated. By combining scale and proportion with findings/solutions on the STEM Wheel, students consider, "To what extent does the scale and proportion of this study impact the results?"

Debatable questions can be posed that require multiple lessons, experiments, or resources throughout a larger unit of study. In order to answer the question, students explore multiple studies, reports, problems/solutions, or experiments. For example, if studying erosion, a question may be asked: "Should we stop natural erosion?" or "How might we stop the overpopulation of an invasive species?" You may purposefully select resources and guide students through inquiry-based experiments or activities that will help students draw their own conclusions using their own experiments and content

TABLE 6.2 Depth question examples by content area

Content	Topics Common in Most State Science Standards	Example Depth Questions to Guide a Unit
Science	Plants	Should we disperse seeds or let nature do the work?
	Ecology	Should humans intervene to control overpopulation of species?
	Geology	Should we stop natural erosion?
	Electricity	Are electromagnetic waves harmful to humans?
	Processes for Investigation	Which method or process is best for investigating ____?
Engineering	Design Thinking	How might we best design a prosthetic limb for an injured animal?
	Processes	What is the best way to create a ____ that ____?
Math	Geometry	Does one's perspective impact the proof that is applied? (e.g., where one stands if calculating distance)
		Are rectangles squares? Are squares rectangles?
	Fractions and Ratios	Are fractions ratios? Are ratios fractions?
	Number and number sense	Is a negative integer a number?
	Problem-solving processes	Which process or method is best for solving the problem? Does the rule or formula work in every scenario? Is there a time when the formula may not work?

provided. Students answer the question by forming a hypothesis and providing evidence for their ideas and individual interpretations. Figure 6.4 shows examples of how multiple resources can be used to explore this question (see also Appendix B2). After examining this question through multiple means, students may revisit the STEM Analysis Wheel to begin planning how to present their conclusions. The organizer can be used to compare experiments, analyze multiple articles or points of view, evaluate different problem-solving approaches (which is the best or most efficient way to achieve the purpose or goal), or to analyze varying perspectives on an issue (e.g., How might an ecologist view the situation differently than a biologist?).

If you are applying the Problem-Reasoning Model in engineering, students might use the model to determine which solution is better. They would create a chart that lists potential solutions and pros/cons for each as they analyze ideas and determine next steps. In math, students could use the model to analyze mathematical problem-solving processes. The "sources" in math, in this example, would be the different methods for problem solving; the point of view or perspective would be that of the student and their selected problem-solving methods, and the implications would be the pros and cons of the different methods used and how well each method works given different scenarios.

Abstractness

Abstractness is the connection of facts to broader ideas such as generalizations, rules, theories, concepts, laws, or principles. The incorporation of abstractness in STEM can be achieved in a variety of ways. You can introduce students to specific generalizations and ask them to connect ideas from a text to those generalizations. A more detailed explanation and examples of generalizations are found in

	Question: Should we stop natural erosion?			
Sources	Textbook information about erosion	Video on the implications of human intervention on the environment	My science experiments on the impact of wind and water erosion	My own ideas or hypothesis
Point of View or Perspective	No, we should not stop natural erosion	Yes, we should stop natural erosion.	Maybe. There are ways to stop natural erosion, but these ways may not be permanent.	
Implications	Natural erosion helps provide nutrients to other areas and can be part of the Earth's cleansing process.	Natural erosion depletes the soil and can cause landslides or other problems that harm living things.	Natural erosion has positive and negative implications for humans and the environment.	
New Ideas or Questions I Have:				
Task	Answer the question, "Should we stop natural erosion?" Incorporate examples from at least two different experiments and one informational text we have examined in class as well as your own research. Create a model to show your thinking and the impact of your conclusion on at least two systems.			

FIGURE 6.4 Problem-Reasoning Chart – STEM example with depth question and multiple sources
Source: Adapted from "Reasoning about a Situation or Event" by Center for Gifted Education, n.d., retrieved from http://education.wm.edu/centers/cfge/curriculum/teachingmodels. Copyright 2015 by William & Mary, Center of Gifted Education.

TABLE 6.3 Universal theme connections in STEM

Generalization – Structure	Science Connection (Unit on Plants)	Math Connection (Place Value)	Engineering Connection (Bridge Design)
Structure promotes function and malfunction.	How does the structure of plants support photosynthesis?	Why does the order of a number matter?	How does the design of your bridge meet the specific criteria outlined? Create a model.
Structures are made up of parts that have functions.	Create a model that shows the various parts of a plant and the function of each. Select one part of the plant structure and explain what would happen if that structure were changed in some way.	What is the difference between base 10 and base 2 when writing numerals?	How will you test each part of your bridge to determine that it is stable?
Structure and function create cause-and-effect relationships.	What is the effect of different climates on the structure of plants? Provide an example.	What happens when you change the order of the numbers in a sequence? How does the number value change?	If you adjust one part of your structure how do the other parts of the structure adapt? What are the positive and negative effects?
Structure + another concept	How does the structure of plants promote the transfer of energy?	What patterns do you notice when subtracting versus adding based on the place value and the structure of the problem?	How do force and tension impact your design?

Chapter 2. Concept maps are another effective tool for encouraging students to organize their ideas and amass facts into broader categories and specific generalizations. In this way students are not just discussing concepts on a general level but supporting specific generalizations with evidence from a variety of sources, experiments, or approaches. Abstractness can be added in STEM by linking facts, experiments, or problem-solving approaches and solutions to already established laws, principles, theories, or mathematical formulas. Students may also test their own hypotheses and approaches and determine their own generalizations from findings and experiments.

Abstractness and Universal Concepts and Generalizations, Theories, and Laws

To add abstractness to STEM fields, students could be asked to complete an organizer that supports their learning about how certain phenomena support a universal theme. Table 6.3 shows ways you can use the universal theme of structure to ask questions that help students make connections to specific topics.

Abstractness and Generalization/Rule/Formula Creation

Abstractness can also be added to lessons by providing students with a word bank of discipline-specific or micro concepts that they must link together to create their own generalization or rule. Table 6.4 shows examples of possible word banks and example generalizations that students might create in different disciplines or STEM fields of study. The creation of generalizations from word banks makes great exit tickets and promotes conversation in scientific discussions. You can also differentiate the task by assigning different words or concepts or by changing the relationships for which students are connecting.

TABLE 6.4 Examples of concept word banks and generalizations

Prompt:
Create a true statement or a generalization about the relationship between (insert the specific discipline or content area) using two or more of the following words/concepts (list concepts) we have studied. Be prepared to model how your generalization is true in multiple contexts and scenarios.

Discipline/Content Area	Concept Word Bank	Example Generalization
Math – Addition and Subtraction	sum, difference, even, odd, multiple, variable	The sum of an even and an odd number is an odd number.
Math – Area and Perimeter	perimeter, area, square, rectangle, triangle, difference, sum, equivalent, greater, smaller	The perimeter of a rectangle will be larger than that of a square if they both have equivalent area.
Science – Matter	matter, space, mass, energy, liquid, heat, solid, gas, molecule, space	Matter takes up space and has mass; energy does not.
Science – Pushes and Pulls	motion, speed, direction, force, collide, change, push, pull	Pushing or pulling on an object can change its speed or direction.
Engineering Processes and Habits of the Discipline	failure, tests, process, design, solution, criteria, costs, problem, structure	Engineers design tests to determine failure points in structures so these can be fixed.

Checking for Understanding

If we teach in a way that encourages higher level thinking and expert thinking, then the tasks and activities that we ask students to complete need to mirror the instruction. Otherwise, how will we be sure that students understand the information presented? So, the tasks, products, and activities are also differentiated by applying depth, complexity, or abstractness in ways that mimic the new instructional tasks and required activities. The following examples in Table 6.5 illustrate how the STEM Analysis Wheel, depth questions, and concepts/generalizations/laws (abstractness) can be used to differentiate products. Differentiating the criteria of the task demand supports expert thinking and cultivates a richer understanding of the phenomena being studied, planned, or designed. Table 6.5 provides examples of grade-level and differentiated tasks in STEM fields when applying features of depth, complexity, and/or abstractness.

TABLE 6.5 Differentiated product tasks by differentiation feature and content area

Grade-Level Standard	Grade-Level Task	Differentiated and Advanced Task	Applicable Features of Differentiation
NGSS 3-PS2–2 "Make observations and/or measures of an object's motion to provide evidence that a pattern can be used to predict future motion." (e.g., swinging on a swing, a ball rolling in a bowl, a seesaw)	Given a set of photos, predict the motion that will continue by drawing arrows to show the path.	Given a set of photos, organize them based on what will happen next and which one of Newton's Laws is best supported based on the motion and principles illustrated.	The task is differentiated by adding abstractness as students link their observation to a law or generalization.
CCSS Math 1.MD.B.3 "Tell time to the nearest hour and half hour using analog and digital clocks."	Given a "toy" clock or clock photo, move or draw the hands on the clock to show (model) specific times at the hour and half hour.	Given a "toy" clock or clock photo, show (model) how time changes when you switch from the hour to half hour by moving forward on the clock (e.g., 7:00 to 7:30 or 7:30 to 8:00). Provide an example for how movement of time from hour to half hour is really the same amount of time.	The task is differentiated by adding complexity as students examine the changes in time.
NGSS MS ETS1 (paraphrased) Evaluate different design solutions to determine how well each meets specific criteria.	Given two scenarios or design solutions for creating a prosthetic limb, students determine which approach achieves the best results based on the specific criteria set forth.	Given two scenarios or design solutions for creating a prosthetic limb, students create a model that shows how different inputs and outputs affect the design and criteria.	This scenario is differentiated by abstractness as students model ideas related to systems (inputs and outputs).
NGSS LS.2.A.2 "Plants depend on animals for pollination or to move their seeds around."	After watching videos and reading a story about seed disbursement, students draw a model to show how plants move their seeds to other areas.	After watching videos and reading a story about seed disbursement, students answer the question: Should humans disperse seeds or let nature do the work?, using information and models from multiple sources.	The task is differentiated by depth. Students are asked to answer a debatable and real-world question from multiple perspectives or resources.

Conclusion

The models discussed in this chapter serve as tools that guide students to understand the complex relationships and patterns among various STEM disciplines and how we can measure, test, model, predict, and explain phenomena or solve problems in the world around us using mathematical and scientific principles. The frameworks provided in this chapter serve as a foundation for students to build a scientific understanding and communicate ideas or create designs through graphs, numbers, models, or creations that are based on specific criteria. Additionally, these models provide a structure for recognizing the relationships between the interconnected STEM disciplines. Such skills are crucial for students as they prepare to explain, test, and solve future problems and ask important questions that support new innovations.

Adding Differentiation Features through STEM Project Choices

The STEM project choices showcase a variety of ways students can demonstrate their understanding of a lesson or unit topic. These ideas are common projects that are often given to grade-level students, but here they are differentiated with complexity, depth, and/or abstractness in order to provide more challenge. Note that you will need to incorporate specific content within the assignments relevant to the lesson or unit's specific content or standards.

- Create a three-minute video documentary that shows how you would model _____ (scientific phenomenon). Incorporate at least two parts of the STEM Analysis Wheel and explain the relationship. (Complexity)
- Develop a poster presentation explaining two sides of a specific scientific principle or issue about _____. Use STEM Analysis Wheel to analyze the principles set forth (Complexity – analysis; Depth – issue to be discussed)
- Create a question that leads to two choices (Should we _____ or _____? Is it better to _____ or _____?) Complete the Problem-Reasoning Chart – STEM to think through the issue, using evidence from your research and scientific principles to consider choices. (Depth)
- Write a rule based on patterns you notice when _____. (Abstractness)
- Select a process for solving _____ and defend why your process is best for meeting your purpose or goal or answering your question. (Depth)
- Given a specific rule or formula, students determine whether or not that rule or formula is true using proofs, models, and examples. (Abstractness)
- Develop a plan for an experiment that answers the question _____. What details are important to include in your study? What information is already known? What has been tried already? What new methods might you employ? How will you show your findings? (Depth – question; Complexity – planning of the experiment using interactions on the STEM Analysis Wheel)
- Develop four questions using interactions on the STEM Analysis Wheel to ask the author of the study you have just read. (Complexity)
- Create an experiment, model, or scenario that illustrates one of Newton's laws. (Abstractness)

Created by Tamra Stambaugh & Emily Mofield, 2022

7

Models for Incorporating Visual Analysis of Art

Why Teach Visual Analysis?

Like language arts, visual art communicates a message through a medium, though the medium is not of words, but of images, brushstrokes, line, and color. Analyzing visual art provides insight into the past and allows us to see the visual creative world of the present with new perspectives. Beyond simply looking at a piece of art and thinking "that's lovely" the skills of visual analysis help students go deeper into exploring questions such as "Why is the art lovely? What is it about the art that creates this reaction? Why am I looking at this art in this way? How has this art impacted others throughout history?" (University of Oxford, 2018). Further, incorporating art analysis within other content disciplines can guide the development of critical interpretation skills.

This chapter provides a model to guide students toward a sophisticated analysis in the visual arts, applying skills of critical interpretation to paintings, sculpture, media, and other forms. The skills in this chapter are somewhat of an extension to the learning skills of a literary scholar or historian. Those who professionally analyze art through a historical perspective do so through a lens of understanding the artist, the techniques and style used, and the historical context, etc. Exposing students to these skills can help them develop an understanding of how an artist crafts an idea just as an author crafts a story. This exposure puts students on a path toward expertise within the humanities as they build upon and apply a framework for understanding how art reflects the culture, emotion, and intellect of the human experience.

Instructional Ideas and Models for Adding Complexity for Analyzing Visual Art

The ideas and content of art interact with the viewer to ignite an intellectual thought, emotion, or connection with culture. How does the artist achieve this? How does a viewer become aware of how to dialogue with the art in such a way as to think about its meaning and value? Adding complexity to art analysis promotes students' understanding of how different features in a piece of art interact in ways that support its message, main idea, purpose, or representation of culture. The Visual Analysis Wheel (Appendix A10) supports this thinking by combining the different features of art (e.g., images, organization, techniques, etc.) with the artist's purpose, point of view, background, and emotional intent in ways that guide students to understand how these features interact to bring meaning to the viewer.

As students become accustomed to using the Visual Analysis Wheel, they can then use it as a tool to think about the development of their own piece of art. For example, they might consider how their intentional use of specific techniques might evoke emotion in the viewer. Using the Visual Analysis Wheel as a model guides students to understand the role of purpose in an artist's technique, use of images, and organization of ideas.

Example: Visual Analysis: **A Sunday Afternoon on the Island of La Grande Jatte** – *Georges Seurat*

In this example, the Visual Analysis Wheel is applied to *A Sunday Afternoon on the Island of La Grande Jatte* by Georges Seurat. Before applying an in-depth analysis to a work of art, ask students to examine specific details in it by asking questions such as, "What do you notice? What's interesting to you? What one word do you associate with this work of art?" Provide background information on the piece to explain that Seurat used small dots of primary colors to create secondary colors (blue and red placed close together look purple from far away). Explain that Seurat was a famous 19th Century French impressionist painter (1859–91) who is widely known for developing and popularizing the techniques of pointillism (small dots of color used to create a scene rather than brush strokes) and chromoluminarism (the interaction of various colored dots to create a more solid impression of color). His pointillism required a mathematical-scientific approach to painting and a strong understanding of the ways in which colors interacted with one another. You may also show a video clip of Seurat's life from biography.com.

Then introduce students to the Visual Analysis Wheel and begin asking simple questions first and recording appropriate responses and then moving to more complex questions and interactions (how one element contributes to, interacts with, or impacts another). It is important to help students see the connections visually by drawing arrows between multiple elements of the wheel.

Simple Questions for Beginning Discussion and Modeling

The following are examples of simple questions to ask in guiding an initial discussion about the text (questions and sample responses adapted from Stambaugh et al., 2018). See Figure 7.1 for an example of how elements of the wheel connect across elements.

- Images: What is the content of this piece? What are the main images that you notice in the painting? Why did the artist choose the subjects that he did? What do you notice about the individuals drawn in the painting? How are they alike and different? What do the individuals' interactions suggest about society at the time? (Ordinary people from all walks of life are seen meeting in a "harmony of opposites.")
- Organization: Where are your eyes drawn to first? How do the subjects and the interaction of light impact the meaning of the work? Why do you think the subjects are placed where they are? (Shows shade and light, 7 x 10 feet – very large for this time period; shows a variety of people; people are straight or sideways; the border is in inverted color.)
- Techniques: What techniques are used by the artist? (Consider how pointillism and the interaction of small primary-colored dots converge to form secondary colors when seen from a distance.)
- Artist's Background: What do we know about Georges Seurat? What is the artist's style? (Remind students of your earlier discussion about his life and pointillism as well as Seurat's interest in science. His work is characterized as neo-Impressionism.)
- Emotions: How do you feel when you see this painting? What are the dominant emotions? How did the artist achieve this? (The people seem rigid and stiff, no emotion expressed.)
- Purpose/Context: When and where was this work of art made? What do you think Seurat's purpose was in making this work of art? (Painted in 1884 in France. His style is considered a more rebellious form of Impressionism – neo-Impressionism. His purpose was to paint modern people who came from all different backgrounds, some poor and some rich, some who worked and some who didn't. The park along the river was where people came to relax on Sundays, and he captured how people interacted on a Sunday afternoon. He was fascinated with the ways things interacted, especially people from different classes, and revealed this through this painting by including subjects who were from differing backgrounds.)

- Main Idea: Based on what we know about Seurat's purpose in painting, what do you think the main idea of this work of art is? (Note: Seurat never revealed an intended main idea. Many critics have suggested that it serves as political commentary of social structures and class in France during the late 1800s. The main idea of the work of art may be to portray a harmony of opposites.)
- Point of View/Assumptions: What is Seurat's point of view about the painting? (Seurat was fascinated by encounters among opposites – city and farm, wealthy and poor – which can be seen spending a Sunday afternoon at the park. He assumes that viewers will see the essence of the piece even though it is not painted with lines, but with tiny dots.)
- Evaluation: Do you like this work of art? Why or why not? (Students may explain a variety of perspectives.)
- Implications: This is a very famous painting. Why do you think this is so? (The artist's use of pointillism and chromoluminarism are innovative ways to produce a work of art.)

Complex Questions for Discussion and Differentiation

The following are examples of complex questions.

- Images + Techniques: How do the interactions of multiple colors through pointillism impact the image? (The interaction of the primary colors allows for an optical illusion of complementary colors.)
- Techniques + Emotion + Images: How do the artist's techniques reveal emotion? (Seurat paints a faceless figure, portraying an idea of anonymity. There is no disorder in the painting, though there are children, and it portrays leisure. Most of the people all have shadows over them. This is somewhat anti-expressive, portraying the people as static or rigid.)
- Point of View + Technique: How does the technique of applying the different combinations of individual dots to form a unified color help us understand what he might be saying about interactions? (Individual people can come together and be unified or interact in positive ways.)

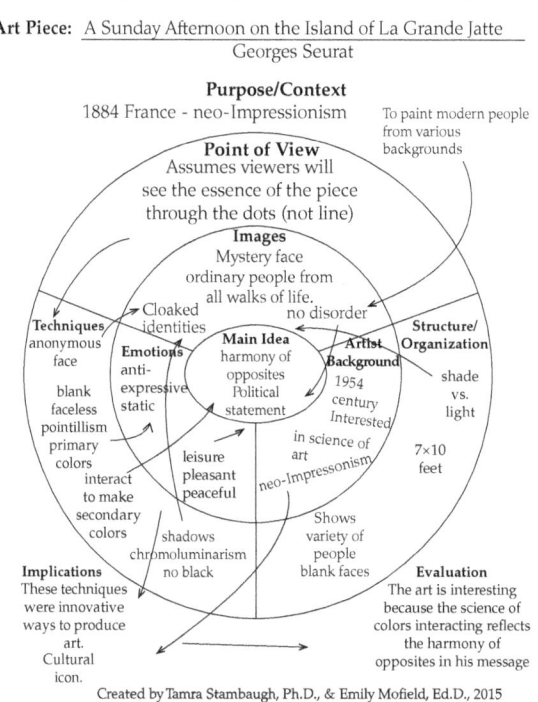

FIGURE 7.1 Example of completed Visual Analysis Wheel – *A Sunday Afternoon on the Island of La Grande Jatte* by Georges Seurat

Other Uses of the Visual Analysis Wheel

The Visual Analysis Wheel can also be applied to other types of visual works including film, advertisements, propaganda posters, and commercials. Using the wheel, students may analyze how a filmmaker uses lighting, frame shots, and portrayal of color as techniques to enhance the ideas in film. Students can also examine how advertisers purposefully use visual elements and images to evoke emotion and how artists of propaganda use content, organization, and visual techniques to influence an audience toward a way of thinking. The Visual Analysis Wheel is similar to the Rhetorical Analysis Wheel (described in Chapter 4) in that students apply a critical interpretation of the artist's (and author's) point of view and assumptions and consider how these relate to the purpose and main message of the piece. Using a slightly different structure, the Visual Analysis Wheel prompts students to focus on the visual elements used for communication of ideas as opposed to textual elements.

Creating Complex and Differentiated Questions Using the Visual Analysis Wheel

The Visual Analysis Wheel provides a framework for thinking about how the elements within the work of art interact to communicate an idea or emotion to the viewer. It can also be used as a tool to differentiate questions, tasks, and assignments. You can design tiered questions that are deliberately differentiated toward increased complexity.

As shown in Table 7.1, Level 1 questions focus on understanding single elements on the wheel. Level 2 questions focus on interactions between two different elements on the wheel, and Level 3 questions combine three elements or encourage divergent thinking by asking students to manipulate elements on the wheel and discuss alternatives. When possible, add specificity from the text into the questions (e.g., how do Seurat's interests influence his technique of pointillism?) as opposed simply asking a question using category names from the wheel (e.g., how does the artist's background influence his techniques?).

Creating Complex and Differentiated Tasks

In addition to asking leveled questions, the following examples illustrate how the Visual Analysis Wheel can be used to create differentiated and complex tasks and activities. We provide several examples in Table 7.2 of grade-level tasks differentiated with complexity. Note that the task demands do not require students to discuss multiple and isolated elements of the wheel in succession but require interaction of the elements. Essentially you are differentiating the criteria of the task demand by asking students to examine more complex relationships that support a richer understanding or expression of art.

TABLE 7.1 Questions with increased levels of complexity: visual analysis

Increasing Levels of Complexity	*Example Questions for* A Sunday Afternoon on the Island of La Grande Jatte *by Georges Seurat*
Level 1: A single element	How does Seurat structure his art? What images stand out as particularly intriguing?
Level 2: Interaction of elements	How does the technique of pointillism develop the idea of a harmony of opposites?
Level 3: Manipulate elements and consider the possibilities or combine interactions among multiple elements	What if this painting were painted with the style of realism instead of neo-Impressionism? How would this affect the perception and emotion of the viewer?

TABLE 7.2 Examples of differentiated complex tasks for visual analysis

Grade-Level Task Example	Task Differentiated with Complexity Using the Wheel Elements
Make your own piece of art with pointillism, using only the three primary colors.	Make your own piece of art with pointillism using only three primary colors to show the idea of harmony and evoke a specific emotion within the viewer.
Compare Van Gogh's *Starry Night* to the song lyrics of "Starry Starry Night" by Don Mclean. What aspects of the art relate to the song?	Compare Van Gogh's *Starry Night* to the song lyrics of "Starry Starry Night" by Don Mclean. How do Van Gogh's artistic techniques (depth, movement, exaggeration) develop ideas and emotions mirrored in the song?
After viewing M.C. Escher's *Relativity*, make your own piece of art with an optical illusion.	After viewing M.C. Escher's *Relativity*, make your own optical illusion to convey an idea about journeys by using techniques and use of structure similar to Escher (e.g., use of impossible realities).
Write a paragraph to explain how the main ideas in Moyo Okediji's *The Dutchman* convey ideas of the trans-Atlantic slave trade.	Write a paragraph to explain how Moyo Okediji communicates ideas of conflict within the trans-Atlantic slave trade through the use of shattering techniques and structure in *The Dutchman*.
Look at the art *Cape Cod Sunset* by Edward Hopper. Write a personal reflection to explain your emotional reaction to the piece.	Look at the art *Cape Cod Sunset* by Edward Hopper. Write a personal reflection to explain how the artist's historical context and use of techniques affect your emotional reaction to the piece.
Look at the art *Improvisation No. 28*. By Vasily Kandinsky. What type of music or specific song would you associate with this work of art and why?	Look at *Improvisation No. 28* by Vasily Kandinsky. What type of music or specific song would you associate with this work of art? Explain by referring to how the artist's assumptions and techniques influence your selection of music.
After viewing the painting *Mont Saint-Victoire* by Paul Cezanne, describe what makes this work of art different from other works of art during this time.	After viewing the painting *Mont Saint-Victoire* by Paul Cezanne, describe what makes this work of art different from other works of art during this time by explaining how various elements of the Visual Analysis Wheel contribute to one another.
Do you like this work of art? Explain why. (Applied to any art)	Do you like this work of art? Explain why by referring to how the artist integrates his/her ideas effectively to you as a viewer by referring to how images, techniques, and organization develop the ideas and evoke emotion.

Depth

Applying depth to analyzing a work of art can be accomplished by asking carefully designed debatable questions. These questions may come in the form of should or forced-choice questions that require students to form an opinion with supporting evidence, justify a stance, conduct additional research to craft a response, or examine various possibilities and perspectives. In analyzing a work of art, evidential support is derived from the viewed art and the inferences students are making about the meaning of the work of art. Once the question is posed, students form an educated opinion or position based on the evidence and details within the work of art. Depth questions are not intended to be judgment-based queries that lack textual or other evidential support but larger, real-world questions that encourage students to form an opinion by interpreting evidence and drawing conclusions based on their own research or analysis. Overall, depth questions prompt students to engage with content deeply in order to adequately support their response.

An example of a depth question for the painting *A Sunday Afternoon on the Island of La Grande Jatte* by Georges Seurat could be "Is this piece more about science or art?" This question encourages students to research more about Seurat's background, his fascination with science as it relates to color, and the cultural context of the time in France. After researching this information, students can justify their inferences with evidence from the painting. Similarly, for the piece *Starry Night* by Van Gogh, the debatable forced-choice question "Does this piece convey hope or despair?" allows students to use evidence from the art (and evidence from the Visual Analysis Wheel) to justify their perspective. Depth questions are useful especially for facilitating Socratic seminars or providing an overarching question for examining the multiple pieces.

Depth Applied to Integrated ELA Standards and Tasks

Questions that promote depth can be posed as debatable questions to support the integration of ELA standards. ELA standards relating to speaking and listening, writing, and literacy about story illustrations can be easily integrated with visual art. As emphasized in Chapter 2, standards may also be accelerated for advanced learners. The chart in Table 7.3 shows how a product or activity related to the

TABLE 7.3 Depth tied to standards and tasks integrated with ELA

Art and Depth Question	Product or Activity and Standard	Specific Task Demand
The Mixed-up Chameleon by Eric Carle Is the mixed-up chameleon still a chameleon? (Illustration where he is all mixed up)	Small-group Discussion CCSS.ELA-LITERACY.RL.1.7 Use illustrations and details in a story to describe its characters, setting, or events.	Students support their point of view using evidence from the story.
Cape Cod Evening by Edward Hopper Are the people happy?	Tell A Story CCSS.ELA-LITERACY.SL.2.4 Tell a story or recount an experience with appropriate facts and relevant, descriptive details, speaking audibly in coherent sentences.	Students examine details in the work of art to create a story to support their ideas about whether the people are happy. After telling their story, they may write their stories.
A Sunday Afternoon on the Island of Grande Jatte by Georges Seurat Is this painting more about science or art?	Short Research Investigation CCSS.ELA-LITERACY.W.3.7 Conduct short research projects that build knowledge about a topic.	Students conduct research about Seurat's life to understand the role of science in his art. They can support their point of view by synthesizing research and evidence from the work of art.
Starry Night by Vincent Van Gogh Does this piece convey hope or despair?	Round Robin Discussion CCSS.ELA-LITERACY.SL.5.1.A Come to discussions prepared, having read or studied required material; explicitly draw on that preparation and other information known about the topic to explore ideas under discussion.	Each student is asked to defend their answer with a new detail from the art (one that has not been previously mentioned).
Still Life with Guitar – Variant State (1913) by Pablo Picasso Is this a guitar?	Explanatory Paragraph CCSS.ELA-LITERACY.W.6.2.B Develop the topic with relevant facts, definitions, concrete details, quotations, or other information and examples.	Students write an explanatory response to describe how Picasso applies techniques that do or do not represent a guitar through sculpture.
The Dutchman by Moyo Okediji Is this painting more about the oppressor or the oppressed?	Opinion or Argument Writing Essay CCSS.ELA-LITERACY.W.7.1 Write arguments to support claims with clear reasons and relevant evidence.	Students write an argument essay to defend their point of view, citing evidence from the art and using the Visual Analysis Wheel.
Relativity by M.C. Escher Does this work of art show that truth is perception or that truth is reality?	Quick Debate CCSS.ELA-LITERACY.SL.8.1.D Acknowledge new information expressed by others, and, when warranted, qualify or justify their own views in light of the evidence presented.	Students stand on opposite sides of the room to defend their response, citing evidence from the work of art.

ELA standard can be addressed by responding to depth questions about visual art. It gives a number of examples of how depth can be incorporated with several ELA standards and task demands.

Abstractness

Concept Maps and Organizers

Abstractness is the connection of facts to broader ideas such as generalizations, rules, theories, concepts, laws, or principles. The incorporation of abstractness in visual arts can be achieved in a variety of ways. You can introduce specific generalizations to students and ask them to connect ideas from a text to those generalizations as indicated in Figure 7.2. A more detailed explanation and examples of generalizations is found in Chapter 2. Concept maps (see Chapter 2) are another effective tool for encouraging students to organize their ideas and amass facts into broader categories and specific generalizations. In this way students are not just discussing concepts on a general level but supporting specific generalizations with evidence from a variety of sources.

Figure 7.2 gives an example of adding abstractness to *A Sunday Afternoon on the Island of LaGrande Jatte*. Students complete the concept organizer explaining how the art supports different generalizations about interactions. Students can continue to add to this handout by applying it to other stories, texts, media, or art.

Checking for Understanding

If we teach in a way that encourages higher level thinking and expert thinking, then the tasks and activities that we ask students to complete need to mirror the instruction. Otherwise, how will we be sure that students understand the information presented? So, the tasks, products, and activities are also differentiated by applying depth, complexity, or abstractness in ways that mimic the more advanced instructional tasks and daily activities.

You can provide a more rigorous task for students by incorporating more than one differentiation feature. As noted in Table 7.4, the grade-level tasks are differentiated by including depth and complexity, complexity and abstractness, or abstractness and depth. This combination allows students to practice multiple applications of expert thinking within the task. Consider a student's readiness and pace of learning when considering the extent to which differentiation features are applied.

Generalizations for Adding Abstractness	*Textual Evidence from* A Sunday Afternoon
Interactions can be positive, negative, or mutually beneficial.	The interactions of individuals within the art are positive, as evidenced by the relaxed and playful interactions in the art. The interactions of color within the technique of pointillism are mutually beneficial in that they create an illusion of complementary colors.
Interactions allow for changes.	The Sunday afternoon interactions between various groups of people can open viewers' minds to change perspectives about divisions in social class.
Interactions are caused by multiple influences.	Seurat uses the technique of pointillism as a way for primary colors to interact. This causes the perception of complementary colors. This interaction of color is caused by how the eye perceives color (and the science of color).
Interactions + another concept	Interactions + Power Positive interactions between different social classes can have a powerful influence on a community.

FIGURE 7.2 Concept Organizer: *A Sunday Afternoon on the Island of La Grande Jatte*
Source: Adapted from Stambaugh et al. (2018), pp. 71–74. Prufrock Press. Used with permission.

TABLE 7.4 Differentiated and advanced tasks with differentiation features: visual art analysis examples

Grade-Level Task	Differentiated and Advanced Task	Applicable Features of Differentiation
Create a summary to describe the techniques used by Hokusai in *The Great Wave off Kanagawa*. Imagine the summary will be displayed alongside the piece of art in a famous art museum.	Create a short written analysis of *The Great Wave off Kanagawa* that supports the idea "patterns reveal structure." In your analysis, explain how the artist's use of framing and mathematics were used to convey ideas. Imagine the analysis will be displayed alongside the piece at a famous art museum.	Complexity is added through the interaction of visual elements (techniques develop the ideas). Abstractness is added through the connection to "structure."
Develop a docent audio explanation for individuals viewing *A Sunday Afternoon on the Island of Grande Jatte*. Describe the use of pointillism and chromoluminarism within the art.	Develop a docent audio explanation for individuals viewing *A Sunday Afternoon on the Island of Grande Jatte* answering the question "Is this piece more about art or science?" Use information about how Seurat's background and context of the time influenced his techniques of pointillism and chromoluminarism.	Depth is added through the incorporation of the forced-choice question. Complexity is added by including the interactions of elements (how background and context influenced techniques).
Create a lesson for younger students to understand the ideas in *Starry Night*. Teach students how Van Gogh conveys emotion.	Create a lesson for younger students that helps students understand the idea "perspective influences interpretation" in *Starry Night*. Teach students how Van Gogh challenges perspectives through the use of specific techniques to convey emotion and create images.	Abstractness is added by focusing the task on an abstract idea – perspective. (Perspectives influence how we perceive the art – Van Gogh's perspective shows the sky as light when in reality it is dark.) Complexity is added by incorporating the interaction of multiple elements (techniques + images + emotions).
In a short essay explain how *Day and Night* by M.C. Escher relates to a short story we have read. Use evidence from the story and work of art to support your response.	Relate the art *Day and Night* by M.C. Escher to a short story we have read as it relates to the idea "There are positives and negatives to realizing the truth." How do the work of art and the short story answer the question, "Is it best to know the truth?" Provide your response in a short essay, citing evidence from both works.	Depth is added through the use of a forced-choice question that requires students to substantiate their claims with evidence from the story and work of art. Abstractness is added by asking students to examine how the idea "There are positives and negatives in realizing truth" is in both works.
Compare a film to a book or novel: How does the film enhance or detract from the author's original intent? Compare the film-maker's portrayal of the story to the author's original portrayal.	Does the film's portrayal enhance or detract from the author's original intent? In your explanation, include how the film's visual elements enhance or detract from the author's original intent. Consider how the film-maker's use of framing, lighting, length of camera shots, angles, and portrayal of color develop the content, emotions, and message of the film.	Depth is added through the use of a forced-choice question that requires students to relate their understanding of the story to the techniques used by the film-maker. Complexity is added by requiring students to discern the interaction of multiple elements, specifically how the film-maker's techniques contribute to the content, emotions, and message.

Integrating Visual Art in Standards

Teaching analysis skills through the visual arts can be valuable in supporting standards within other subjects, especially ELA. Students can understand the parallels when they analyze how authors communicate ideas through the organization and techniques applied to language while artists communicate ideas through the organization and techniques applied to images. In many ways, art can be considered a "text" in which students make inferences from evidence. Students can discuss and write about the conclusions they draw from their analysis of the work of art as they would an analysis of text. Including a work of art as a comparative piece within a unit of study can also help students examine how big ideas, themes, and abstract concepts are portrayed through a variety of genres, texts, media, and art. Table 7.5 shows how various differentiated tasks for art analyses relate to content standards, especially in ELA.

TABLE 7.5 Differentiated tasks integrated with ELA standards

Differentiated Art Task or Activity	Relating to Standards	Explanation of Differentiation Features(s) and Integration of Standards
How do the ideas in *Cape Cod Sunset* by Edward Hopper relate to the character Ivan in *The One and Only Ivan* by Katherine Applegate? In your explanation, discuss how the idea "interactions can be positive, negative, or mutually beneficial" relates to each piece.	CCSS.ELA-LITERACY.RL.2.3 Describe how characters in a story respond to major events and challenges.	Abstractness is included by asking students to relate both the art and the text to the concept generalization of interactions. Students relate the character interactions and associated emotions to the art.
How do the ideas in *Improvisation No. 28* by Kandinksy relate to the emotions of Rachel in the story *Eleven* by Sandra Cisneros? In your written response, explain how Kandinksy's use of structure and techniques (color, line, form) evoke emotion within his painting.	CCSS.ELA-LITERACY.W.5.9 Draw evidence from literary or informational texts to support analysis, reflection, and research.	The task includes complexity because it requires students to examine the interaction of multiple elements (organization + techniques + emotion). Students draw inferences from both the story and the art in a short writing task.
How does *The Subway* by George Tooker relate to the main ideas in *The Lottery* by Shirley Jackson? In your response, explain how the artist and author would answer the question "Is ignorance bliss?" citing evidence from the art and text.	CCSS.ELA-LITERACY.RI.6.7 Integrate information presented in different media or formats (e.g., visually, quantitatively) as well as in words to develop a coherent understanding of a topic or issue.	Depth is incorporated through the forced-choice question. Students must examine the evidence to defend their point of view with evidence from the art and text. Students must integrate information from two forms of text (visual art and a text) to answer the depth question.
Examine the painting *The School of Athens* by Raphael. How does this art reveal the essence of the Renaissance? Explain how the content, organization of the art, and use of visual depth are used to convey the idea "Progress leads to more progress."	CCSS.ELA-LITERACY.RH.6–8.2 Determine the central ideas or information of a primary or secondary source; provide an accurate summary of the source distinct from prior knowledge or opinions.	Abstractness is included by linking the task to the concept of progress. Students must apply their historical background knowledge to understand the content and central ideas in the art. They can use the Visual Analysis Wheel to organize their thinking to answer the question.
Examine German propaganda in World War II using the Visual Analysis Wheel. How does the artist's techniques and point of view contribute to evoking emotion within the intended audience?	CCSS.ELA-LITERACY.RH.6–8.6 Identify aspects of a text that reveal an author's point of view or purpose (e.g., loaded language, inclusion or avoidance of particular facts).	The task includes complexity because students must explain the impact of elements (techniques and point of view on emotion). Students view the art as "text" to examine point of view.

Conclusion

The Visual Analysis Wheel serves as a tool for students to analyze art as an integrated whole, including discerning the content and style of the art and how the art is situated within historical context and culture. This framework builds a content base for learning about art and provides a structure for recognizing the relationships between visual elements, context, and the viewer's interpretation. When visual art analysis is integrated with other content such as ELA or social studies, students can sharpen their skills of communicating and critiquing ideas of intellectual and cultural value.

Creating Interdisciplinary and Intradisciplinary Connections

While experts bring domain-specific knowledge to solving problems, most real-world issues require an interdisciplinary approach that includes multiple perspectives and ideas from a variety of disciplines. Interdisciplinary learning allows students to make cross-disciplinary links and uncover patterns in a number of contexts and situations. As we prepare students to encounter present and future issues related to climate change, social justice, health problems, and emerging technologies, we can plan learning experiences where students examine the intersections between various disciplines. Through an interdisciplinary approach, we can bring coherence to curriculum by encouraging students to integrate their knowledge from a variety of topics and sources, discover insightful connections, and create new ideas from these intersections.

Interdisciplinary learning involves the overlap or intersection of multiple disciplines, while intradisciplinary learning involves staying within the boundaries of a discipline while connecting various domains of the discipline. An example of intradisciplinary learning in ELA might include linking a literary analysis applied to science fiction to an argument writing assignment about human interactions with changing technologies. An example for science content might include examining the structure of matter in science and later guiding students to discover the same conceptual abstract connections when studying the structure of anatomy.

In this chapter, we present a number of ideas for planning interdisciplinary and intradisciplinary units around concepts and issues that cut across domains and perspectives. When designing units or inter and intradisciplinary connections we recommend beginning with an overarching debatable question (depth) that cuts across the disciplines targeted or integrated to a universal concept, theory, or law (abstractness) that supports the connections being made. Then apply the appropriate accelerated texts and content (acceleration) with content-specific wheels (complexity) to analyze texts and visuals or plan for products. We provide multiple examples next.

Using Overarching Questions to Make Inter and Intradisciplinary Connections

The use of overarching questions can be used to guide students in making inter and interdisciplinary connections. We suggest the overarching questions be designed with depth or abstractness.

- ◆ **Depth:** Think of a broad debatable question that would include multiple perspectives, disciplines, and resources. For example, a question such as "Was the Industrial Revolution more progressive or destructive for society?" allows students to examine how various disciplines,

DOI: 10.4324/9781003238515-8

authors, texts, and/or research findings support an argument. At the end of the unit of study, students can synthesize their learning to answer the question with evidence and reasoning.

◆ **Abstractness:** Plan units around a concept such as change, systems, power, truth, etc. and create an overarching question that allows students to link various perspectives, disciplines, and resources. For example, you can play with the generalizations "Equilibrium is the balance of competing forces" or "Equilibrium can be static or dynamic" and create a driving question such as "How is equilibrium achieved?" As students complete a series of lessons, they should be able to synthesize their learning from various sources to develop a conclusion.

Interdisciplinary Connections

Science and Social Studies Connections: Ocean Trash

In this example, students study the real-world problem of ocean trash (the Great Pacific Garbage Patch) by examining it through both a science and a social studies lens. First, a depth question is posed at the beginning of the unit to guide student inquiry, "Is the problem of ocean trash reversible?" Students are introduced to the problem by watching a video about the impact of the ocean trash on the Galapagos Islands. Students might first use the STEM Analysis Wheel as a type of KWL organizer, noting what they have learned and what they want to learn more about after watching the video. They would first note separate elements and then make connections between multiple elements on the wheel. Additionally, you might ask a few guiding questions, both simple and complex, in class discussion to discuss the many causes and effects of the problem.

In Table 8.1, there are student recorded notes from the video. From here, students could write additional insight, background knowledge, and other questions on the wheel in a different color ink (e.g., if there are microplastics in fish, how does this affect humans?) (Note, not every element of the wheel is noted in this example but could be). As students discuss these components, guide them to make connections across the wheel with arrows. For example, students can link processes/methods to findings/solutions, noting that once scientists determine the type of plastic and where it is from, it leads them to know the type of solution (e.g., address the manufacturer of the plastics directly).

After exploring this problem from a science perspective, students could watch the video again and use the Social Studies Connections Wheel to consider social causes and effects of the ocean trash.

TABLE 8.1 Student notes from *Plastic in Paradise: The Battle for the Galapagos Islands' Future*

STEM Analysis	Student Notes from Video (Students Write on Wheel)
Idea/Hypothesis/Question	Scientists are asking, "Where is the trash coming from? How will we solve the problem?"
Cause and Effect	Caused by mismanagement of waste Caused by overuse of plastics Affects wildlife and locals Affects future citizens
Patterns	Scientists are able to determine the cause through examining where the trash came from (and what type)
Scientific information	Ecosystems, food chains; physical science (structure of matter)
Scale and Proportion	We can only see 1% of the trash in the ocean. Microplastics are difficult to measure (we eat, breathe, drink tiny particles). We must understand the scale of rubbish per person.
Perspectives/Audience	Residents; marine biologists
Evidence/Data	Collect evidence on type of plastic, where it is from, and how it travels
Processes/Methods	Using drone technology and algorithms to analyze plastic items; use software to determine how plastic travels in water

Examining the same video in this lens drives the idea that though the problem is a result of human behavior, individuals have the power to impact change. Then, students could watch additional videos and read articles to continue to add notes to the wheel to gain more insight into understanding the problem. A few examples of students' notes and questions on the Social Studies Connections Wheel are provided below:

- Geography: What areas of the world are contributing the most to the trash here?
- Economics: Plastics are cheap and easy to make. Businesses make more money from making large quantities of cheap goods.
- Innovation: The innovation of plastic makes life easier (introduced after WWII as light, durable material).
- Culture: Disposing items after one use is the norm.
- Social Structure: Citizens are not aware of the long-term consequences of one-use disposable plastics.
- Politics/Power: The laws in various states are different (e.g., banning plastics bags); lack of consistency across the globe.

Students then might make connections across the factors and generate their own questions:

- Politics/Government + Innovation: How can laws be used to incentivize new innovation?
- Economics + Politics/Power: How might we create policies to inhibit manufacturers from making plastics?

TABLE 8.2 Interdisciplinary study on ocean trash through the concept of systems

Overarching Question	Depth Question: Is the Problem of Ocean Trash Reversible?			
Lesson topic	Intro to ocean trash	Sustainable solutions	Recycling myths	Effects on ecosystems
Resource	Video: *Plastic in Paradise: The Battle for Galapagos Islands' Future*	Video: *Can these Companies Solve the Plastic Waste Problem?*	Articles about myths of recycling	Articles about the effects of microplastics on marine life
Use of Depth and/or Complexity	Use STEM Analysis Wheel and Social Studies Connections Wheel to identify causes and effects of the problem. Portrays the effects are profound but reversible if we know the source.	Students add to the wheels and also debate, "Are bioplastics a promising solution?" Portrays promising solutions through mushroom packaging	Students examine evidence for "Is recycling worth it?" Students use the Social Studies Connections Wheel to determine the causes of the recycling problem, its effects, and potential solutions. The idea of recycling is causing more of a problem then helping; to reverse the ocean trash, manufacturing must change.	Use STEM Analysis Wheel to discuss long-term effects on the ocean's ecosystem. The effects of plastics on marine life are devastating and long-lasting as they affect food chains, etc.
Abstractness	Link to systems generalizations using concept organizer. Systems include inputs, outputs, elements and boundaries. Systems interact. When one element of a system changes the other elements of the system adapt.			
Differentiated Product	Culminating Project: Create a public service announcement that answers the question "Is the problem of ocean trash reversible?" with specific evidence and appeals. Use the Rhetorical Analysis Wheel to plan your announcement, using evidence from videos, readings, and other research and incorporating interactions between the various elements on the wheel. Incorporate at least one "systems" generalization with your announcement.			

As students read various articles or watch videos, they can examine other depth questions more specifically related to portions of the unit. For example, quick debates, the Choice-Reasoning Chart – Humanities (see Appendix B1), Problem-Reasoning Chart – STEM (see Appendix B2), or argumentative writing can be used as students think through questions such as "Should state governments ban plastic bags?," "Is recycling enough to solve the problem?," or "Are bioplastics a worthy solution?"

In applying abstractness, students can examine the issue through the lens of systems using the concept organizer or a concept map (see Appendix C1). Specifically, students can articulate how the problem of ocean trash relates to a large system of inputs, outputs, parts, and interactions.

Finally, in a culminating assessment, students answer the overarching depth question in a public service announcement. They use the Rhetorical Analysis Wheel (Appendix A5) to craft their argument with supporting evidence learned from the series of videos and articles. Table 8.2 shows a summary of an interdisciplinary study on ocean trash linked to the big idea of systems.

Multiple science and social studies connections abound as science has social implications and social issues often require scientific input.

Using Macro-Concepts or Universal Themes across Multiple Disciplines

When using a macro-concept such as systems, you can plan instruction so that students can integrate other learning from other content areas as well. For example, a team of sixth grade teachers who teach in various content areas can intentionally plan units around the idea of systems. In this way, the content is connected through a conceptual thread so that students see patterns and relationships across disciplines. Table 8.3 shows an example of how units of study from multiple content areas connect through the concept of systems.

Creating Complex Interactions and Interdisciplinary Connections

The analysis wheels can be combined in ways to support student understanding in multiple disciplines. Students can examine complex interactions between elements of each wheel or discipline and then use arrows (or string and tape if using a working wall) to make connections between disciplines. In this way students gain a deeper understanding of multiple disciplines. For example, students may examine a speech using the Rhetorical Analysis Wheel and then apply the Social Studies Connections Wheel to study what was going on during the time the speech was written or to more deeply analyze the events that were referenced in the speech. The order of this could also be switched depending upon the context (e.g., Social Studies Connections Wheel and then speech). Examples of other connections are found in Table 8.4.

TABLE 8.3 Macro-concept of systems cutting across multiple disciplines

Generalization	*Ocean Trash (Science)*	*Great Depression (Social Studies)*	*Central Tendencies (Math)*	*ELA (Science Fiction)*
Systems interact with other systems.	Interaction of aquatic and weather systems	Interaction of economic and social systems	Interaction of number systems (quantitative data) with real-world systems	Interaction of literary elements to mirror implications of technology on societal systems
When part of a system breaks, the other parts are threatened.	When one element of an ecosystem is affected, it affects food webs and ecological balance.	The stock market crash affected the overall economic structure which impacted housing prices, deflation, and unemployment rates.	When outliers are included in data analysis, the mean is especially affected, influencing skewness in the distribution of data. This affects data analysis inferences about the mean.	When a character experiences a conflict due to technology in the story, this affects subsequent parts of the plot and the overall theme.

TABLE 8.4 Complex connections by combining analysis wheels

Literary Analysis Wheel + Social Studies Connections Wheel	Students make a double timeline of the events in an historical fiction novel and have a separate timeline of the actual historical events that took place during the time period. They create connections to the Literary Analysis and Social Studies Connections Wheel for the book and actual events, showing at least three interactions for each.
	The Social Studies Connections Wheel can be used to understand the impact of a certain piece of political literature (e.g., *The Jungle* by Upton Sinclair) on other social studies factors. Regarding *The Jungle*, this innovative journalism led to social change through the development of new laws and policies.
STEM Analysis Wheel + Social Studies Connections Wheel	Students discuss the social, political, and economic impact of vaccines and connect those to the STEM Analysis Wheel, modeling how vaccines are designed and their effectiveness over time.
	Students create and analyze an engineering design using the STEM Analysis Wheel and then apply the Social Studies Connections Wheel to discuss the implications of the design and the resulting innovation on at least two additional factors on the wheel.
STEM Analysis Wheel + Rhetorical Analysis Wheel	Students complete the Rhetorical Analysis Wheel after reading an editorial about invasive species and then complete the STEM Analysis Wheel to determine the impact of invasive species on the environment.
	Students complete the Rhetorical Analysis Wheel to analyze an editorial science cartoon and then complete the STEM Analysis Wheel to determine the scientific implications and accuracy of the cartoon concepts exploited.
STEM Analysis Wheel – STEM + STEM Analysis Wheel – Math	Students use their knowledge of fractions and proportions to create scale models of their engineering design; students use the STEM Analysis Wheel to plan their design to scale.
Literary Analysis Wheel + STEM Analysis Wheel	Students read *A Wrinkle in Time* by Madeleine L'Engle and complete the Literary Analysis Wheel based on the novel, noting the interactions between various elements; then they complete the STEM Analysis Wheel to determine the accuracy of concepts about astronomy listed in the novel, by creating a question to investigate from the novel.
Rhetorical Analysis Wheel + Social Studies Connections Wheel	Students apply the Rhetorical Analysis Wheel to a historical speech such as "Ain't I a Woman" by Sojourner Truth. To add more contextual understanding to this speech, students would also apply the Social Studies Connections Wheel to understand how various factors such as social structure, economics, geography, government, and world context affected Sojourner Truth, and in turn, how Sojourner Truth impacted various factors.

Integrating Multiple Disciplines by Adding Depth Questions

Debatable questions can be posed that would require multiple lessons, texts, or resources throughout a larger unit of study, connecting art and poetry interpretations. For example, an overarching question for a unit might be, "Is truth perception?" or "Is change positive or negative?" You may purposefully select pieces that reflect a number of perspectives or sources on the issue. Students answer the question by forming an opinion and providing evidence for their ideas and individual interpretations. Table 8.5 gives examples of how multiple art pieces and poetry can be used to explore "Is change positive or negative?" After examining this question through multiple sources and perspectives, students write an opinion piece that incorporates examples from the three selected texts and their own research, thus adding complexity through the examination of interactions among various elements and interactions among different text selections (i.e., different perspectives).

Similarly, Table 8.6 shows how science videos and simulations coupled with fictional and nonfiction texts are used to answer the question: "How do humans impact the ecosystem?" After students finish their investigation and complete the chart, they create a podcast or PowerPoint presentation to discuss how humans impact the environment and whether the impact is positive or negative, using examples from at least three different sources in the unit.

TABLE 8.5 Overarching question for unit with art and literature connections

Overarching question	Is change positive or negative?			
Text/Art	*School of Athens* by Raphael (painting)	"I like to see it lap the miles" – Emily Dickinson (poem)	"Nothing Gold Can Stay" – Robert Frost (poem)	*Still Life with Guitar – Variant State* (1913) Pablo Picasso (sculpture)
Possible response	Positive – the great thinkers from the past come together with those from the present (of the time) to share ideas that bring positive change to innovation and thought.	Positive and negative – new technology brings destruction but also progress.	Change is negative in that something is lost, but change is positive in that each stage of change leads to growth (leaf subsides to leaf).	Is the change to abstract art from realistic art positive or negative? (Depends on viewer perspective)
Culminating assignment	Write an argument essay that answers the question, "Is change positive or negative?" Incorporate examples from at least three different texts or art we have read and viewed in class. Be sure to provide specific textual examples to support your argument.			

TABLE 8.6 Overarching question with science and literature connections

Question: How do humans impact the ecosystem?				
Sources	*Picture Book:* The Great Kapok Tree By Lynn Cherry	Pros of Deforestation	Wild Boars Video/ Information	Food Web/Food Chain Simulations
Perspective/ Point of View	Humans should protect the environment for the future.	Humans can use the environment for survival – especially renewable resources.	Humans need to intervene to keep overpopulation of animals from destroying the producers (O2).	Ecosystems work to remain in balance but can get out of balance if too many of the same species are present.
Assumptions	Man is destroying the future.	We need certain resources for survival; renewable resources will grow back or repopulate.	Wild boars will continue to destroy food sources for other animals and upset the balance.	Humans may help or hurt food webs and food chains but these chains work to remain in balance.
Implications	Humans can help or hurt ecosystems depending upon their involvement. They need to think about the future as well as the present when making decisions. They need to know about ecosystems and how different living and nonliving things within the ecosystem interact.			

Source: Adapted from Stambaugh et al. (2018). Prufrock Press. Used with permission.

Planning Interdisciplinary Units

Interdisciplinary unit planning takes time initially but also allows more time for instruction when content is taught in conjunction and not in isolation. Additionally, multiple content standards can be combined and taught at once. As previously mentioned, we recommend starting with an overarching depth question or concept and then applying the wheels to further analyze the texts, experiments, or other content necessary for abstractness or in-depth analysis. Finally add the specific content wheels for complexity and combine them.

We find it helpful to select one discipline or topic to get started. If you are an elementary teacher and you teach all subject areas, perhaps you begin with science or social studies content. Then investigate possible real-world issues or debatable questions that are grade-level and context appropriate to guide the unit. After that, select applicable fiction and nonfiction texts or videos that provide multiple perspectives to answer the question. Table 8.7 shows an example of this planning in ecology and literature. When planning this unit, the science topic was selected first (food webs and food chains). Then debatable questions were selected and focused on specific lessons. An overarching question was also selected (see Table 8.6). Then fiction and nonfiction resources in ELA and science were found related to the debatable questions and content standards and include various perspectives, resources, and other information. The specific subject activities were matched to the appropriate analysis wheels. An overarching concept and generalizations of interactions were embedded, and products (based on standards and outcomes) were designed with criteria to show depth, complexity, and abstractness.

TABLE 8.7 STEM/ELA Unit Planning Example

What Accelerated Content and Resources Will I Use?	*What Depth Question Might We Discuss?* (See Table 8.6 for an example of how this column may be applied)	*How Can I Add Complexity in ELA?*	*How Can I Add Complexity in Science?*
Picture Book: *Great Kapok Tree* by Lynne Cherry	Should we cut down trees for shelter? (Add text to Reasoning Through A Situation – STEM)	Literary Analysis Wheel with complex connections	Connections to content outlined in the text to the STEM Analysis Wheel with complex connections
Article: Pro and Con Perspectives on Deforestation Text	Should we cut down trees for shelter? (Add text to Reasoning Through A Situation – STEM)	Argumentative Analysis Wheel with complex connections to examine arguments of each side of the issue	Connections to content outlined in the text to the STEM Analysis Wheel with complex connections
Simulations, Videos and Models on Food Webs and Food Chains	Should we cut down trees for shelter? (Add text to Reasoning Through A Situation – STEM)	Text Analysis Wheel to review the information from the video and make connections to various elements on the wheel	STEM Analysis Wheel to analyze simulation video and make complex connections to various elements on the wheel

How Can I Add Abstractness?

Which Concept/Generalizations, Theories or Laws Match the Content?

The concept and generalizations of interactions was chosen for this unit. After each lesson, students add information and newly learned facts to a concept map working wall that lists the generalizations of interactions.

Students also link new concepts such as ecosystems, relationships between humans and the environment, food webs, and food chains, and overpopulation of species to the concept of interactions and write new generalizations.

How Can I Add Authentic Products with Criteria?
What products are required by my content standards and content experts and practicing professionals? What criteria are necessary to help students create a complex or in-depth product?

Depth/Complexity Product Example:
Create an opinion speech, podcast, or other mode of communication that best explains your response to your selected debatable question from the unit or another approved question you have. Use evidence from at least two sources used throughout the unit. Use the Argumentative Analysis Wheel to plan your response along with scientific information and connections from the STEM Analysis Wheel.

Abstractness Product Example:
Which generalization about interactions best describes how food chains and food webs work within an ecosystem? Use specific examples to explain your answer.

Source: Adapted from Stambaugh et al. (2018). Prufrock Press. Used with permission.

Conclusion

The use of depth questions, overarching themes/generalizations/theories or laws, and multiple analysis wheels to examine interactions within and between disciplines provides a strong infrastructure for creating inter or intradisciplinary units. Examine your standards across multiple disciplines and, if permissible, reorder the standards in ways that allow you to make connections. Creating these opportunities for students to examine the intersections within and between content domains opens doors for insightful connections, innovative ideas, and new questions for inquiry.

9

Making Differentiation Work: Additional Considerations

In this chapter we share some principles to consider when implementing the models discussed throughout this book in your classroom to support students' ongoing talent development and expertise. What we present is not a comprehensive list, but ideas for incorporating the models in your setting while remembering that students are at the forefront of differentiation practices. One of the main goals is to support students' educational endeavors, strengths, interests, and talents in content-specific domains. We want to help students fall in love with a content area with which they may eventually choose to engage in more in-depth ways, eventually providing creative contributions in their field.

Use Data to Determine Curriculum Match, Strengths, and Interests

Use data to match learning to a students' prior knowledge, interest, and skills. Strategies such as curriculum compacting (pretesting and excusing students from previously learned material as a way to buy time for more rigorous opportunities, questions, and study) allow students to work at a pace and level that is appropriate for them. We must also remember that some students may not have had the exposure necessary to obtain high scores on assessments but can learn information at a faster pace once exposed and be ready for more in-depth, complex, and abstract work more quickly after exposure.

The models shared in this book can be used to differentiate questions and activities, support flexible and skill-based groups, or be used as a template for designing extension activities, tiered assignments, or in-depth research opportunities for students who have shown mastery of and deep interest in certain aspects of the grade level curriculum. However, providing options for choice or interest alone is not as powerful as providing choice and pursuit of interest with differentiated content and models that cultivate depth, complexity, and abstractness.

Provide Specific Feedback

Provide specific and targeted feedback that supports students moving to the next level on the learning and talent development continuum. Feedback is an important part of expertise development (Bransford et al, 2000). When providing feedback, use the models and frameworks presented in this book as a guide. For example, in social studies if a student were writing an essay about a specific historical event, the wheel could be used to pose new interactions for the student to discuss, if this were not part of the original submission, helping students realize the interactions between various elements that influenced an event or person. The following questions can help you think through the specific feedback you need to provide:

- What is the goal or outcome?
- To what extent was the goal or outcome met?
- What criteria am I using to know whether or not the goal or outcome was met?
- What does the next level of mastery or expertise look like? What are the steps? How can I communicate and guide students to attain the next level?
- What models can I use to help me frame my feedback (e.g., connections on the wheel)?
- What are the top one or two most important things for the student to focus on for the most growth?

Make sure the feedback is specific and targeted to the content. A good rule of thumb is to provide a specific comment about what was done well and then provide a next step or idea to consider, guiding students to move to the next level of understanding in the content area (even if the next step is beyond the current grade level expectation or standards). Instead of simply saying "Great job! Your answers were clear and concise," provide a specific comment about a component of the work such as "You provided a detailed explanation for how the setting and characters influenced the conflict in the story. Now connect that information to the theme of the text." In this way, students know what they did well and where they need to go next. In this instance, the Literary Analysis Wheel was used as a guide for feedback and next steps. Debatable question components or conceptual development and generalizations can also be used to guide feedback and next steps within a content area. Conversations about student work with immediate feedback or guides for reflection are also important. Table 9.1 lists some sentence stems that may be helpful for giving feedback and for guiding a deeper understanding of the content, supporting processes, or correcting misconceptions.

Define Terms and Create a Common Schoolwide Language for Differentiation

Definitions matter. Work with others in your school to provide common definitions for words like differentiation, depth, complexity, or abstractness and provide models to support the common language. Too often we use words like complexity, for example, as part of a pedagogical practice but when asked to define it or explain what it looks like in the classroom we are at a loss or the definitions of teachers and administrators vary. The models and definitions introduced in Chapter 2 can be used as an entry point for discussions around differentiation for students who are academically advanced. The definitions can also be used to guide accountability measures or as a reflection of teaching. Figure 9.1 shows how the definitions and features of models can allow teacher reflection or serve as a springboard for conversation

TABLE 9.1 *Feedback question stems for discussions*

Content Feedback	Process Feedback	Correcting Misconceptions through Feedback
What did we learn that . . . ?	How might you. . . .	What about when . . . ?
How does . . . relate to . . . ?	What would happen if . . . ?	Explain more about how. . . .
What do you know about . . . that will help you . . . ?	How does this show . . . ?	Would this be true if . . . ?
Go back to . . . and. . . .	Add/explain/omit . . . and. . . .	Re-examine . . . and. . . .
What do you mean by . . . ?	What if you . . . ?	
	Model how you will. . . .	

Indicator	Yes	No	N/A
Students discussed relationships between multiple events, concepts, or elements in the discipline with supporting details. (Complexity)			
Developmentally appropriate and debatable questions were examined through a variety of perspectives, resources, or variables. (Depth)			
Students linked newly learned content to a specific theory, law, or generalization (or created their own generalizations by connecting two or more concepts into a true statement). (Abstractness)			
Products were provided that included specific criteria appropriate for the discipline and typical in the field. (Authentic Products with Criteria)			
Standards, content, and/or resources were appropriately matched to the students' experience and readiness levels. (Acceleration)			

FIGURE 9.1 Checklist for differentiation using definitions and models as a guide
Source: From Stambaugh (2013).

starters during classroom observations and coaching. Ideally, when a differentiation feature is mentioned, everyone in the school should be able to define it and cite an example or model for implementing it in their content area. Moreover, this provides teachers with the confidence to discuss with parents how they are meeting the needs of students who require more advanced instruction.

Use the Models to Design Reflection Checklists and Assessment Criteria

The models outlined in this book can also be used as a guide for designing assessments and checklists for grading and for guiding students' self-editing of their own work. Use the criteria and definitions of each model to create criteria for rubrics, adding specificity by subject area. For example, if applying complexity to ELA you might create a rubric with the following goal: *Student provides accurate and extensive evidence from the text that shows how at least two different literary elements interact to support the theme.* Similarly, with depth, the criteria or rubric goal could be: *Student accurately synthesizes multiple responses/experiments/ideas to answer the question or solve the problem citing extensive evidence from all sources.*

Likewise, a list of questions can be provided for students to check their work before submitting it. Examples of questions are taken from the criteria for depth, complexity, and/or abstractness. Here are a few ideas:

- Did I answer the question completely? (all)
- Did I incorporate multiple perspectives or ideas into my solution or response? (depth)
- Did I show relationships between multiple elements and how they work together to _____? (complexity)
- Did I provide specific facts to support the theory or law? (abstractness)
- Is my generalization accurate when applied to multiple settings? (abstractness)

Teach Affective Skills Necessary for Succeeding in a Talent Domain

A significant part of developing talent and expertise includes helping students master the skills and habits of experts that are necessary to succeed in a given field. Knowledge is important but so is perseverance, mindset, and the ability to effectively communicate ideas (Subotnik et al, 2011). In the following text box, we outline some ideas for infusing habits of a discipline within various content fields. These habits can be taught from early childhood and through adulthood.

Ways to Embed Habits of the Discipline in Curriculum Tasks

- Encourage students to submit work to authentic competitions. Preparing for authentic audiences can often provide the spit-and-polish motivation to improve work.
- Invite mentors or other content experts to provide critical feedback to student work so that students get used to the review process involving feedback, critique, and evaluation.
- Encourage critical peer review so that students become accustomed to criticism and learn how to respond appropriately.
- Develop communication skills so that students can learn to advocate for their own ideas (in writing, in interpretation) even in the face of rejection.
- Cultivate incremental beliefs in student's abilities to communicate ideas. If students convey the idea "I'm just not good at this" encourage next steps toward applying a specific strategy and mindset such as growth over time.
- Focus on and encourage effort and perseverance with tasks when challenging.
- Encourage realistic goal setting, helping students work towards short and long-term accomplishments.
- Normalize the learning process by explaining that learning happens from mistakes.
- Help students become aware of their own strengths and weaknesses through practice with challenging material and exposure to a variety of content-based options.
- Provide biographies or invite guest speakers from diverse groups to the classroom so that students can see others who they can relate to working in a field of study.

Multiple Differentiation Components Can Work Together to Increase the Level of Challenge

For some students, simply adding depth, complexity, or abstractness singularly is not rigorous enough. The Integrated Curriculum Model (VanTassel-Baska, 1986), which we adapted and used as the overarching framework for this book (see Chapter 2), is "integrated." Thus, the more elements discussed here that are added to the curriculum, the more rigorous the task or question. Table 9.2 shows how different

TABLE 9.2 Examples for combining multiple differentiation elements to create more rigorous tasks

Single Element Examples	Combined or Integrated Element Examples
Complexity After reading Plato's The Allegory of the Cave describe how the figurative language and symbols interact to promote the theme.	*Complexity + Depth* Is perception reality? Consider how Plato would answer this question and justify your response by including evidence from The Allegory of the Cave including at least three different relationships between literary elements that together support your response.
Depth Synthesize at least three sources we discussed from class, to answer the question, Should we cut down trees for shelter? Use evidence to support your answer	*Depth + Abstractness* In an essay, answer the question, Should we cut down trees for shelter? Include multiple sources in your response and be sure to connect your response to at least two generalizations about systems.
Abstractness Review the events of 9/11. Explain which generalizations of freedom are most evident based on the events that led to the attacks.	*Abstractness + Complexity* Review the events of 9/11. Select at least two relationships on the Social Studies Connections Wheel (e.g., geography + culture) and discuss how the interactions you chose support a generalization about freedom.

Source: Examples adapted from previously published curriculum units; see Figure 9.2.

elements and components of the curriculum can be combined to add more challenge. Remember that experts are able to combine and synthesize multiple elements (complexity) into categories and conceptual underpinnings (abstractness) in order to solve real-world problems (depth).

Start with One Model and Discipline at a Time; Determine Anticipated Responses First

As educators, we can be quite ambitious in wanting to support our students and meet their unique needs. Learning and applying these models with fidelity takes time, practice, and reflection. Consider selecting one model in one discipline initially, applying the model to a couple of lessons or a unit at first. Understand that the first few times you teach the model it may not go as smoothly as intended. Eventually, with ongoing use, the models will become second nature and guide your thinking and questioning as much as your students. We also recommend that you create questions, determine anticipated responses, and even complete the assignment you are giving to students ahead of time. This exercise helps you better understand the model and guide student thinking or processes when teaching. It also helps you figure out how to scaffold and break down complex and in-depth processes as students are learning the models as well.

Try Ready-Made Examples and Resources that Apply the Models if Needed

We have created several ready-made units in select content areas that incorporate the models and frameworks described in this book. Pilot studies and anecdotal feedback from educators suggest that teaching a ready-made unit first sparks new ideas for applying the models to other content in their grade level. This practice can also reduce cognitive overload as you do not have to apply new content to models while simultaneously learning how to teach a new model. Figure 9.2 outlines some of the ready-made units that can be used as a guide for further exploration. Of course, you can just as easily use the models and strategies discussed through this book with your own content, to create lessons and units given the ample examples provided.

Don't Forget Your Students When Planning Academically Advanced Lessons and Units

Teaching the most rigorous and evidence-supported curriculum does not matter if we forget *who* we are teaching. Scholarly habits (e.g., perseverance, mindset), readiness, experience, race/ethnicity, culture, income level, background, and prior learning opportunities – to name a few – impact how our students engage (Olszewski-Kubilius et al., 2018). A student's interest in a topic, their access to experts in a field, and their level of motivation and opportunities accessible and taken also matter (Subotnik et al., 2011).

We differentiate because we understand that students come to us with different experiences, knowledge, interests, strengths, cultures, and access to opportunities. We recognize students for who they are and where they are in their learning journey. Because students enter classrooms with various readiness levels, you may need to provide scaffolding to students as they engage with these models. Ultimately, we want to support and develop student strengths and talents. We want every student to be more knowledgeable and excited about learning at the end of the school year than at the beginning. The curricular experiences we create using the models and definitions provided in this book are best tailored to student strengths and interests. For example, we can help students turn a topic of interest into a debatable question in a field that they want to study. We can also provide them with resources about the lived experience in social studies or ELA in ways that are relevant and capture the concepts

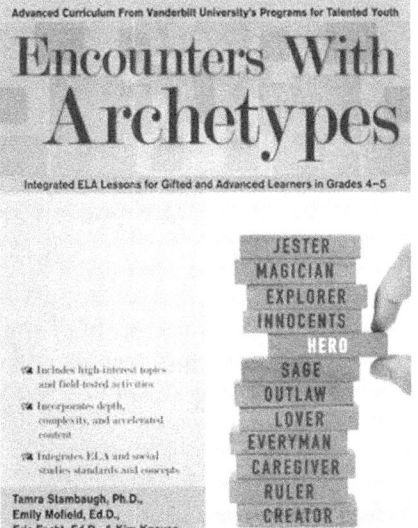

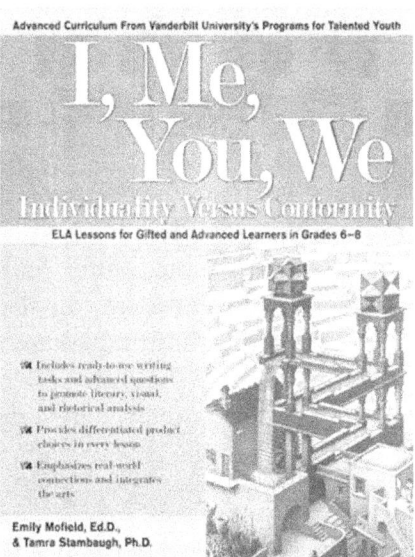

FIGURE 9.2 Curriculum units that incorporate the models discussed in this book

of importance to our students and the curriculum, while also exposing them to other people, places, events, and resources with which they may be unfamiliar.

Use Culturally Responsive Teaching Practices

We must also remember to be culturally responsive in approaching how students learn with these models. Culturally responsive teaching includes teaching students to value their own cultural heritage and those of others (Gay, 2018). To be culturally responsive, we must commit to investing in learning more about students' personal lives, including their interests and cultural backgrounds. It is important to select resources and materials that are representative of diverse perspectives, cultures, and traditions in order to give students opportunities to see themselves in the characters or individuals presented within a given discipline. Additionally, culturally responsive pedagogy includes considering the extent to which the materials allow students to critically examine real-world issues and actions and to make their learning relevant. As we have described, one way this can be facilitated is through depth questions that necessitate examining an issue from multiple perspectives and making connections to macro-concepts such as systems, power, patterns, and change. Our teaching practices must allow students to bring their unique selves to the classroom experience. One of the most important responsibilities we have as educators it to create pathways and learning experiences for students to show their strengths and develop their talents; this talent trajectory begins with a respectable and welcoming classroom for all.

Conclusion

The models and examples in this book serve as a guide for supporting students on their journey towards developing expertise and creative production in a field. When we expose students to the key disciplinary ways of knowing, thinking, and doing as an expert through engaging with meaningful curriculum, we give students opportunities to discover and develop their potential. Curriculum designed in this way enables students to uncover insightful connections, examine critical issues, ask important questions, and link new knowledge to generalizable contexts. Such experiences can have a profound influence on students' lives as they may come to realize they have a strength in a given area. As educators, we can pick up on these strengths and provide contexts to nurture their emerging talents so that students thrive in their learning and future pursuits.

Appendices

Appendix A Models for Complexity: Blank/Annotated Wheels

Appendix A1

Introduction to Using Analysis Wheels

How to Use the Wheels

When using a content-based wheel for the first time with students, start out by asking simple questions about each element and then ask more complex questions by combining elements and/or manipulating them. As you ask students questions, write student responses on the wheel. As students make connections between the elements, be sure to note these connections with an arrow.

If you are emphasizing a particular standard as part of the lesson, then you can focus instruction on how the one element affects other parts of the wheel. For example, if the lesson is focused on characterization, then you can intentionally develop questions that combine all parts of the Literary Analysis Wheel with "character" (e.g., How do the character's actions and thoughts influence the theme? How does the author use language to develop the character? How does the setting affect the character's actions?).

Once students become accustomed to using the wheel, apply a gradual-release approach that moves from teacher-led modeling in a whole group setting to small group work and individual completion with follow-up discussions. This allows students the opportunity to make their own connections and practice thinking without guidance.

Ideas for Using the Wheel

- ◆ Ask students to complete the wheel on their own in preparation for a lesson or Socratic seminar with an overarching depth or concept-based question (e.g., Should animals be kept in zoos? How do encounters lead to threats and opportunities?).
- ◆ Create an interactive wheel using a brad fastener and a paper plate to show how the inner circle turns so that students can examine relationships from inner and outer circles as well as relationships between adjacent elements.
- ◆ For younger students, write each element on the face of two cubes. Students roll one cube and respond to how the text supports that element. Students may also roll two cubes and discuss how the two elements are related or interact. If the same word comes up on both cubes, students may ask the author their own question about that feature or pose an "I wonder" question about that feature.
- ◆ For digital use, type in the elements of the wheel into *Flippity* or other interactive software for students to make connections between elements.

Stambaugh, T., & Mofield, E. (2022). *A Teacher's Guide to Curriculum Design for Gifted and Advanced Learners: Advanced Content Models for Differentiating Curriculum.* Routledge.

Other Tips

- Remember that the wheels are not simply worksheets. They are models for thinking. It is not necessary for students to complete a wheel for every text or lesson. Students can grow weary of completing a wheel over and over again. Remember to use the wheel as a planning tool for asking questions and embedding complexity in an assignment.
- It is not necessary to explicitly teach all components of the wheel before analyzing a text or studying a topic. Focus on relevant aspects of the wheel or take a moment to teach that content and continue the analysis.
- Keep a wheel posted in the classroom on a bulletin board or poster. Students can write responses for various aspects of the wheel on sticky notes to place on the poster.
- When applicable, provide opportunities for students to add to their wheels over the course of a unit. This is especially helpful in more long-term units related to social studies and science.
- When applicable, students can note what they already know about the topic and what they learned about it (from reading articles or watching videos). Then they can use the wheel to pose new questions to explore from the connections made (as this mirrors what experts do).
- Guide students to understand that the elements of the wheels work as parts of systems. When one element is changed, it usually affects all the other parts.

Stambaugh, T., & Mofield, E. (2022). *A Teacher's Guide to Curriculum Design for Gifted and Advanced Learners: Advanced Content Models for Differentiating Curriculum.* Routledge.

Appendix A2

Literary Analysis Wheel – Primary and Literary Analysis Wheel

Literary Analysis Wheel – Primary (K-2)

Examples of Simple Questions

- **Character**: What are the values and motives of the characters? What evidence supports this? How does the author reveal character?
- **Setting**: What is the time and place of the story?
- **Feelings of Author (Tone) and Reader (Mood)**: What are the author's feelings toward the subject (tone)? With what attitude does the author approach the theme (tone)? How do you feel as a reader? Why? (mood)
- **Point of View**: What is the narrator's point of view (first person, third person objective, third person limited, third person omniscient)?
- **Use of Words/Techniques**: What figurative language and imagery does the author use? What is the author's style?
- **Conflict/Problem:** What are the significant internal and external conflicts of the story? What is the main problem? What are the causes and effects of the problem?
- **Theme**: What is the author's main message that can be generalized to broader contexts? (The theme is the author's point of view on a given subject.)
- **Sequence/Plot**: What sequence of events occurs in the story? When and how is the conflict resolved?

Examples of Complex Questions

- **Setting + Feelings of Author (Tone) and Reader (Mood):** How does the setting affect the reader's feelings?
- **Setting + Conflict:** What conflicts could only happen in the setting? How does this influence the plot and theme?
- **Character + Feelings of Author (Tone) and Reader (Mood):** How do the character's actions and responses establish emotion in the reader?
- **Point of View + Conflict/Problem:** How does the narrator's point of view affect the way the reader views the significant conflict and plot events?

- **Theme + Sequence/Plot:** How does the theme impact the development of the plot? If the author wanted to show a different theme, how would he/she have to change the plot of the story? How would the characters' values, motives, and actions change?

Literary Analysis Wheel (Grades 3–12)

Examples of Simple Questions

- **Character**: What are the values and motives of the characters? What evidence supports this? How does the author reveal character?
- **Setting**: What is the time and place of the story?
- **Tone**: What is the author's attitude toward the subject? With what attitude does the author approach the theme?
- **Symbols**: How do objects or names represent more abstract ideas?
- **Point of View**: What is the narrator's point of view (first person, third person objective, third person limited, third person omniscient)?
- **Language/Style/Structure**: What figurative language and imagery does the author use? What is the author's style?
- **Plot/Conflict**: What are the significant internal and external conflicts of the story? What are the significant parts of the plot?
- **Mood**: What is the feeling the reader gets from the story? How is this established?
- **Theme**: What is the author's main message that can be generalized to broader contexts? (The theme is the author's point of view on a given subject.)

Examples of Complex Questions

- **Setting + Mood:** How does setting affect the mood?
- **Symbols + Theme:** How do symbols develop the theme?
- **Symbols + Setting:** How is the setting symbolic of a larger idea (e.g., twilight, autumn)?
- **Character + Mood:** How do the character's actions establish the mood?
- **Tone + Plot:** How is the author's tone revealed in the plot and conflicts? What specific textual evidence supports this?
- **Point of View + Character:** What character thoughts or feelings are revealed or hidden because of the narrator's point of view? How does this impact the reader's experience of the story?
- **Language/Structure + Mood:** How does the author's style and sentence structure enhance the mood?
- **Theme + Plot:** How does the plot affect the theme? How would the theme change if key parts of the plot or ending were changed?

Stambaugh, T., & Mofield, E. (2022). *A Teacher's Guide to Curriculum Design for Gifted and Advanced Learners: Advanced Content Models for Differentiating Curriculum.* Routledge.

BLANK LITERARY ANALYSIS WHEEL—PRIMARY

Directions: Draw arrows across elements to show connections.

Text: _____

- Feelings of Author (Tone) and Reader (Mood)
- Use of Words/Techniques
- Sequence/Plot
- Setting
- Conflict/Problem
- Characters
- Theme
- Point of View
- Structure and Style
- Interpretation

Created by Tamra Stambaugh, Ph.D., & Emily Mofield, Ed.D., 2017.

LITERARY ANALYSIS WHEEL—PRIMARY GUIDE

Directions: Draw arrows across elements to show connections.

Text: _____

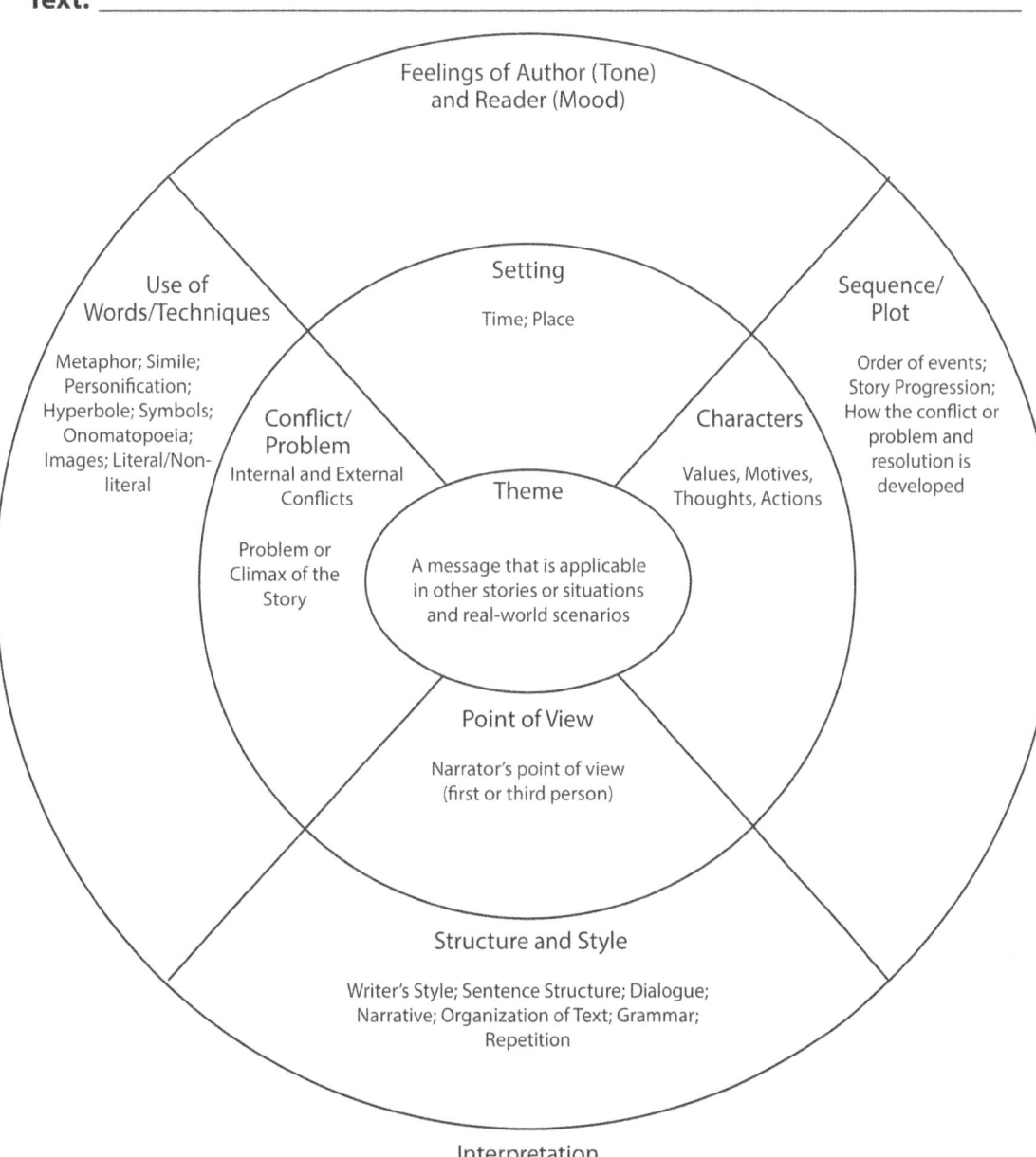

Created by Tamra Stambaugh, Ph.D., & Emily Mofield, Ed.D., 2017.

BLANK LITERARY ANALYSIS WHEEL

Directions: Draw arrows across elements to show connections.

Text: _____

Purpose/Context

- Setting
- Mood
- Language Structure Style
- Symbols
- Plot/Conflict
- Characters
- Theme
- Point of View
- Tone

Interpretation

Created by Tamra Stambaugh, Ph.D., & Emily Mofield, Ed.D., 2015.

LITERARY ANALYSIS WHEEL GUIDE

Text: _____

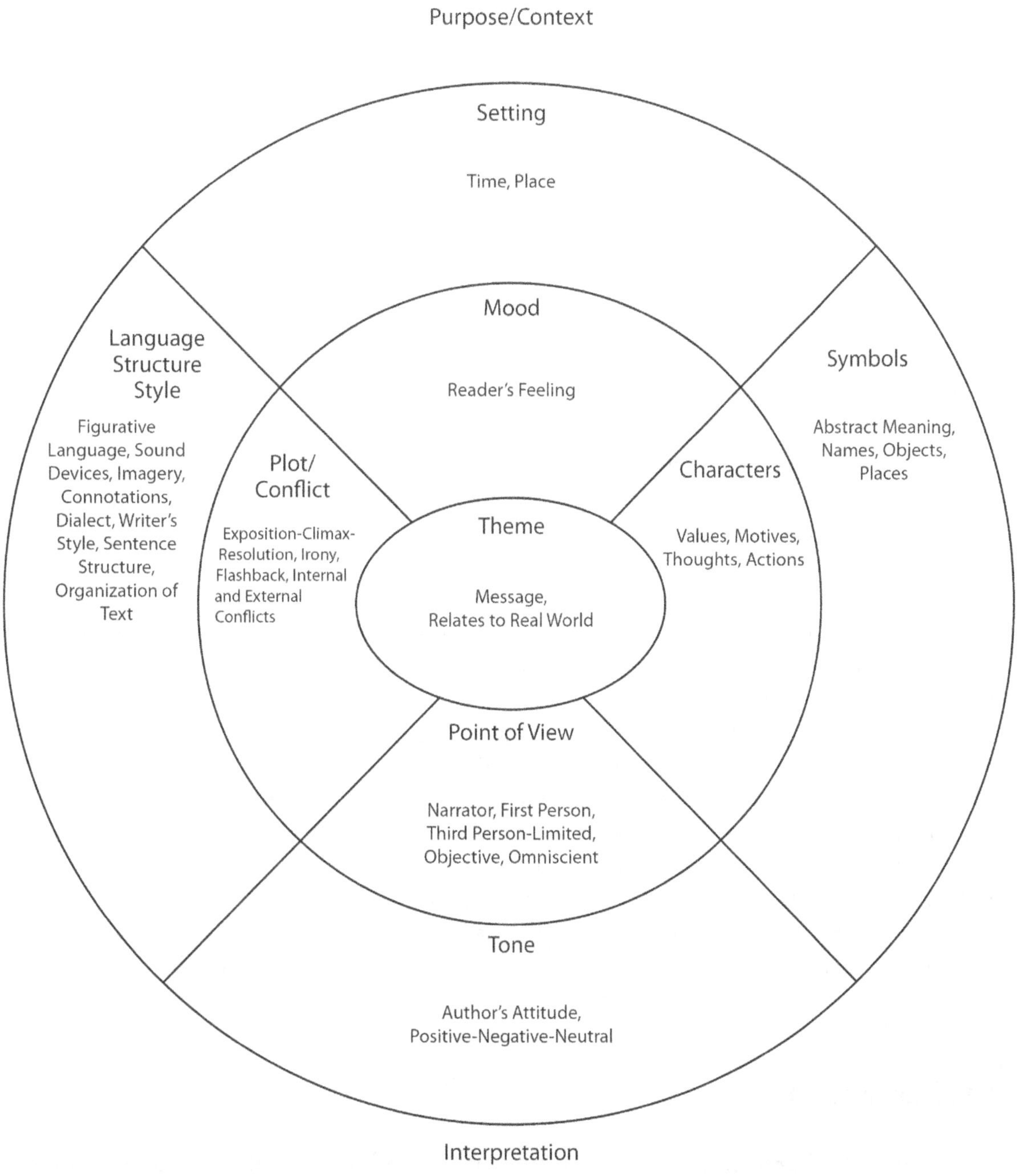

Purpose/Context

Setting

Time, Place

Mood

Reader's Feeling

Language Structure Style

Figurative Language, Sound Devices, Imagery, Connotations, Dialect, Writer's Style, Sentence Structure, Organization of Text

Symbols

Abstract Meaning, Names, Objects, Places

Plot/Conflict

Exposition-Climax-Resolution, Irony, Flashback, Internal and External Conflicts

Characters

Values, Motives, Thoughts, Actions

Theme

Message, Relates to Real World

Point of View

Narrator, First Person, Third Person-Limited, Objective, Omniscient

Tone

Author's Attitude, Positive-Negative-Neutral

Interpretation

Created by Tamra Stambaugh, Ph.D., & Emily Mofield, Ed.D., 2015.

Appendix A3

Fictional Writing Wheel

Examples of Simple Questions

- **Characters/Perspective**: Who is the story about? Who are the major and minor characters? What motivated the characters? What do they want? What do they need? How do they spend their time? Do they like how they spend their time? What do they feel? What do they think? What do they dream about? What are the characters going after versus what do they actually need (theme)?
- **Setting**: Where is the story located? In what time period is the story set? What makes the setting unique?
- **Purpose/Message/Shifts**: Why are you writing this? What message do you want to convey? Do you want the story to be humorous/scary/sad? What important shifts/changes occur to convey the message? What is the theme of the story? What lesson is revealed through the characters and the shifts and conflicts they face?
- **Encounters/Problems/Obstacles**: What people, places, events, or situations are encountered in the story? What effects do these have? Are these always external, or are there internal encounters, problems, and obstacles that the main character has to overcome?
- **Organization and Time:** How is the story structured in a way that reveals who the main character is, what the ideas are, and how the needs of the character are met? How much time passes in the story? How will you frame your beginning, middle, and end?
- **Techniques:** How is figurative language such as similes, metaphors, dialogue, grammar, punctuation, and imagery used to convey your message? What words will you use to explain the character or narrator's attitudes in a way that makes the character relatable (tone)? What words will you use to help readers feel a certain way (mood)?
- **Point of View:** Who is telling the story, a narrator or a character? Will the narrator know everything that goes on (third person omniscient) or only a few ideas (third person limited)? Will a character tell the story (first-person point of view)? If so, which character?

Examples of Complex Questions

- **Techniques + Character**: How can you use similes and metaphors to help the reader understand how your character feels?
- **Purpose/Message/Shifts + Setting + Character:** How does a shift in the setting help the reader better understand the character's perspective? How does the transformation of the character reveal the message or theme of the story?

Stambaugh, T., & Mofield, E. (2022). *A Teacher's Guide to Curriculum Design for Gifted and Advanced Learners: Advanced Content Models for Differentiating Curriculum.* Routledge.

BLANK FICTIONAL WRITING ANALYSIS WHEEL

Directions: Draw arrows across elements to show connections.

Text: _____

Purpose/Context

- Structure, Organization, and Time
- Encounters/Problems/Obstacles
- Point of View
- Setting
- Purpose/Message/Shifts
- Characters/Perspectives (Motivation)
- Techniques

Created by Tamra Stambaugh, Ph.D., & Eric Fecht, Ed.D., 2018.

FICTIONAL WRITING ANALYSIS WHEEL GUIDE

Directions: Draw arrows across elements to show connections.

Text: _____

Purpose/Context

Structure, Organization, and Time

How much time passes in the story? How did the author frame the beginning, middle, and end? Did the author begin with the setting, the obstacle, or the characters and how they spend their time?

Encounters/Problems/Obstacles

What people, places, events, or situations are encountered? What effects do these have?

Point of View

Who is telling the story (the character, a narrator)? What is the point of view (first person, third-person limited, third-person omniscient)?

Setting

Where does the story take place? What makes the place unique? Is there a specific time period?

Purpose/Message/Shifts

Why did the author write this? What message did the author want to convey? Did the author want the story to be humorous... scary... sad? What important shifts/changes occur to convey the message?

Characters/Perspectives (Motivation)

Who is the story about? What motivates the characters? What do they want? What do they need? How do they spend their time? What do they feel? What do they think about their setting?

Techniques

How did the author use figurative language, such as similes, metaphors, dialogue, grammar, punctuation, and imagery, to convey his or her message? What words did the author use to explain the main character's or narrator's attitudes in a way that makes the character relatable (tone)? What words did the author use to help readers feel a certain way (mood)?

Created by Tamra Stambaugh, Ph.D., & Eric Fecht, Ed.D., 2018.

Appendix A4

Text Analysis Wheel – Primary

Examples of Simple Questions

- **Main Idea or Message**: What is the main idea or message of this text?
- **Point of View:**
  - What is the author's point of view toward the topic?
  - What other points of view or texts need to be considered?
  - What facts are included? Are these accurate? What opinions are
  - included?
  - How does my point of view differ or agree with the text?
  - Is this fact or opinion? What biases might be present?

- **Techniques/Structure:**
  - How is the information structured? What techniques are used?
  - How does the author use emotions or story to help convey meaning?
  - How does the author use arguments or facts to help convey meaning?
  - How does the author use or refer to experience or expertise to help convey meaning?
  - What can you learn from the headings, illustrations, charts, or graphs?
  - How does the author explain cause-effect relationships? How does the author show comparisons, sequencing, chronological order, problem/solution ideas, or basic information?
  - How does the author show the relationship between people, events, and ideas?

- **Context/Audience/Purpose:**
  - When was this written? Is this current? How do you know?
  - What is the purpose of this text? Who was this written for?
  - What words do you need to know, define, or draw in order to understand the text?

- **Supporting Details**: What details are used to support the author's message or main idea? Why are these details important to include?
- **Implications**: What are the implications of ___? What are the short-term and long-term implications? Positive and negative implications?

Examples of Complex Questions

- **Point of View + Supporting Details**: What details reveal bias? Do some of these details make you change your point of view?
- **Context/Audience/Purpose + Techniques/Structure**: How does the author's use of emotion, argument, or expertise/experience help the audience understand the main idea? How do these elements support the author's purpose?

BLANK TEXT ANALYSIS WHEEL—PRIMARY

Directions: Draw arrows across elements to show connections.

Text: _____

- Point of View
- Supporting Details
- Techniques/Structure
- Supporting Details
- Main Idea or Message
- Supporting Details
- Context/Audience/Purpose
- Implications

Created by Tamra Stambaugh, Ph.D., & Emily Mofield, Ed.D., 2017.

TEXT ANALYSIS WHEEL—PRIMARY GUIDE

Directions: Draw arrows across elements to show connections.

Text: _____

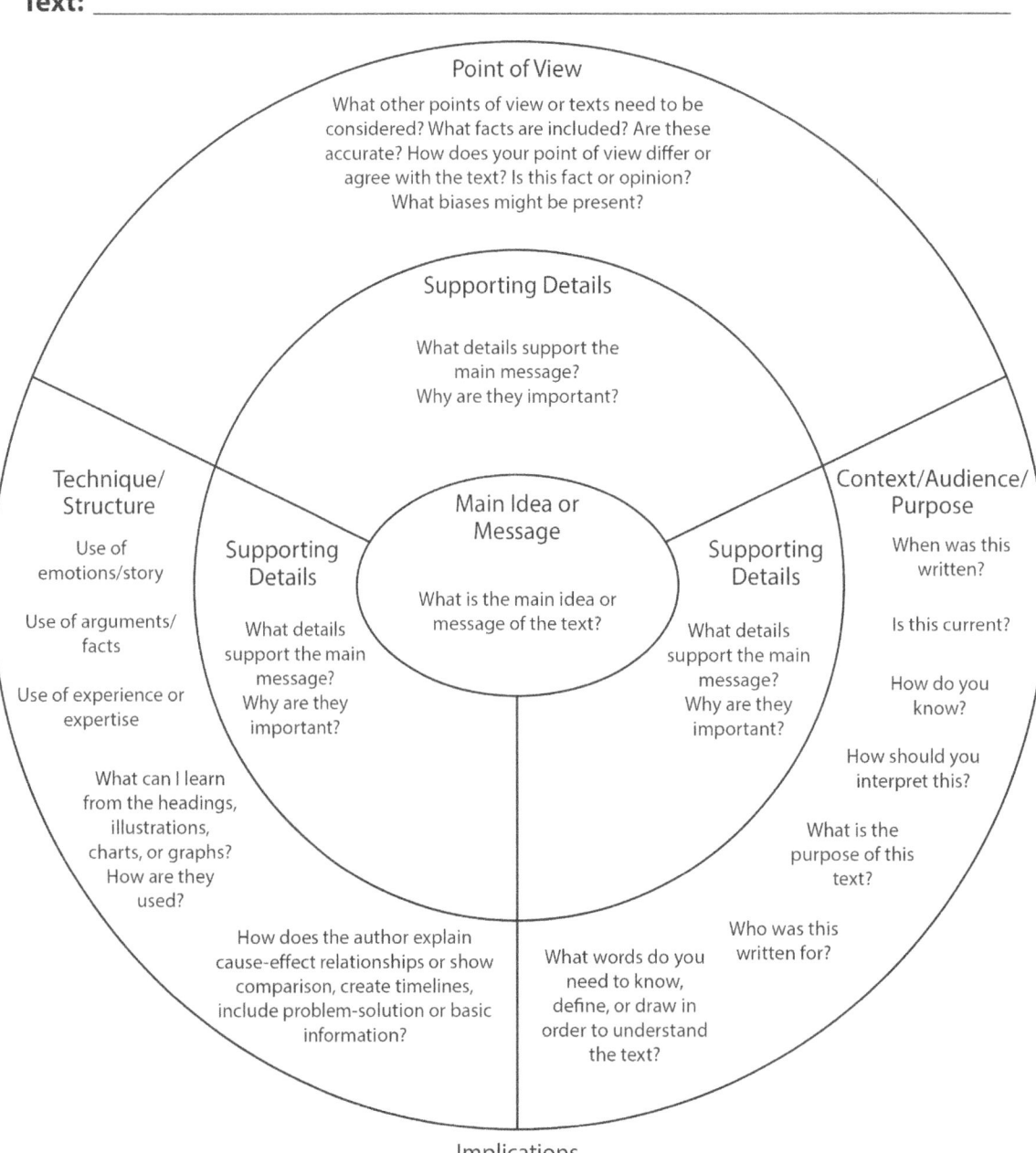

Created by Tamra Stambaugh, Ph.D., & Emily Mofield, Ed.D., 2017.
Some questions are adapted from the CCSS for ELA (National Governors Association for Best Practices & Council of Chief State School Officers, 2010).

Appendix A5

Rhetorical Analysis Wheel

Examples of Simple Questions

- **Purpose**: What is the author's purpose?
- **Context/Audience:** Who is the audience and what is the historical situation? What is the main problem in the historical context?
- **Claim**: What is the main claim or message of the text?
- **Techniques**: What specific techniques does the writer use to develop his/her claim?
- **Point of View/Assumptions**: What is the writer's point of view toward the topic? What assumptions does the writer make? What is the writer's unstated premise or belief? What does the writer take for granted about the audience?
- **Structure/Organization**: How does the writer organize ideas (e.g., problem/solution, point by point, chronologically, sequentially, compare/contrast)? Where is the thesis? Why is it here? Does the writer structure his message deductively or inductively?
- **Logos (Focus on Text)**: What reasoning is used to help the argument make sense? What are the main points? Are statements easy to accept or does the writer need to provide more evidence? What research, facts, statistics, or expert opinions are used? Are these sufficient?
- **Pathos (Focus on Audience)**: How does the writer appeal to the audience's emotions (guilt, fear, pride, etc.)? What word connotations or imagery does the writer use to evoke emotion in the audience?
- **Ethos (Focus on Writer)**: Is the writer credible? How does the writer establish trust? Are sources credible? Does the writer respect an opposing viewpoint? Does the writer address a counterclaim? How? How does ethos help the writer establish an effective argument?
- **Implications**: What are the short-term and long-term consequences of this document?
- **Evaluation**: How effective is the writer in developing his/her claim? To what extent is the purpose fulfilled? Is there a balance of pathos, ethos, and logos appeals? Is there too much bias or emotional manipulation? Is there adequate evidence to support the claim(s)? Is the evidence credible, rational, and organized logically?

Examples of Complex Questions

- **Logos + Structure:** How does the structure of the document help the writer's argument make sense?
- **Pathos + Technique:** What techniques does the writer use to evoke emotion in the audience (e.g., repetition, similes, hyperbole, symbolism, rhetorical questions)?

Stambaugh, T., & Mofield, E. (2022). *A Teacher's Guide to Curriculum Design for Gifted and Advanced Learners: Advanced Content Models for Differentiating Curriculum.* Routledge.

BLANK RHETORICAL ANALYSIS WHEEL

Directions: Draw arrows across elements to show connections.

Text: _____

Purpose/Context

- Point of View
- Logos
- Techniques
- Pathos
- Claim
- Ethos
- Structure/Organization
- Implications
- Evaluation

Created by Emily Mofield, Ed.D., & Tamra Stambaugh, Ph.D., 2015.

RHETORICAL ANALYSIS WHEEL GUIDE

Text: _____

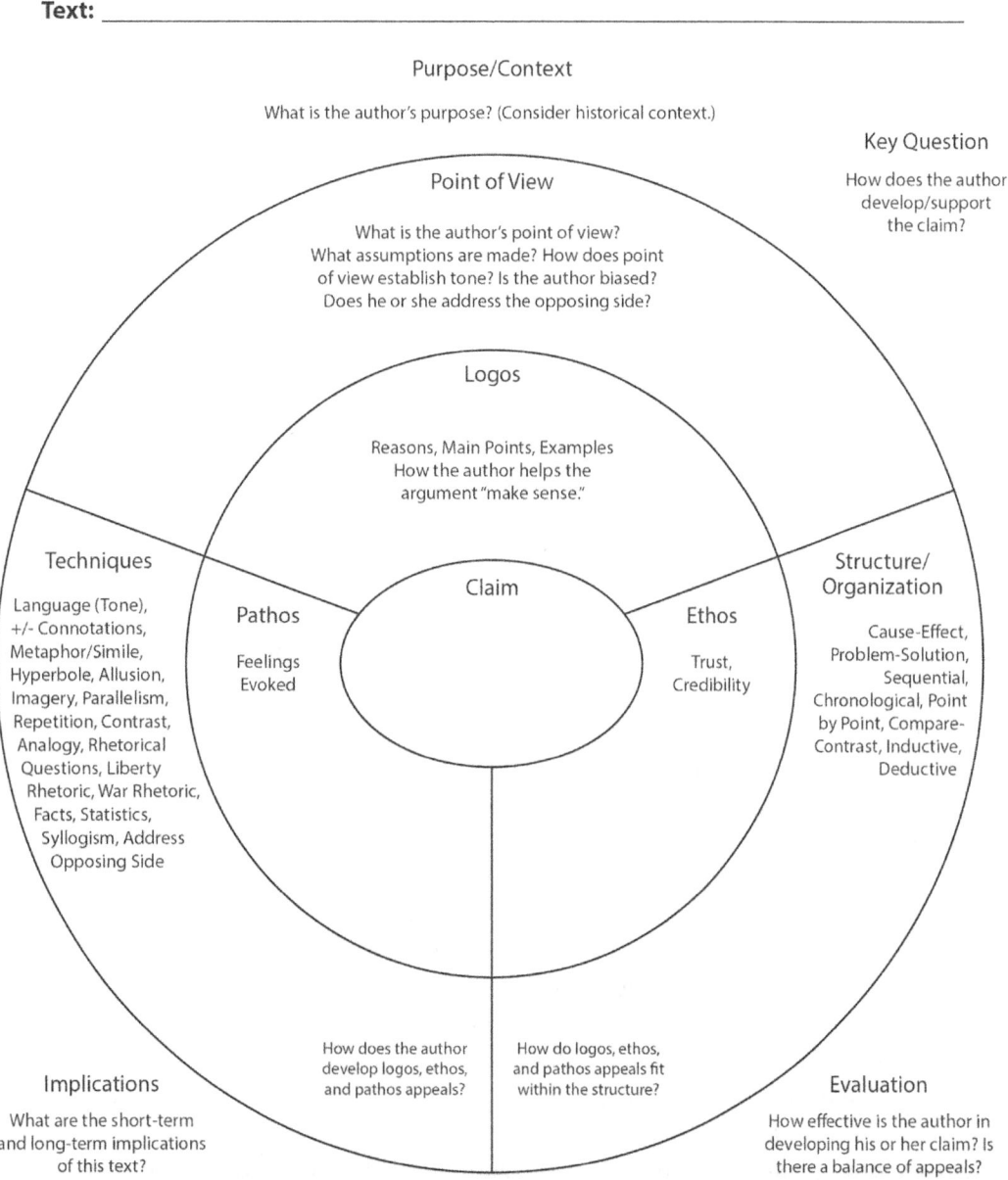

Created by Emily Mofield, Ed.D., & Tamra Stambaugh, Ph.D., 2015.

Appendix A6

Argumentative Writing Wheel

Note that the guiding questions below can be used to analyze argumentative writing and also as a guide for students to craft their own arguments. Questions in italics can be used by students to support their planning.

Examples of Simple Questions

- **Purpose/Claim:** What is the author's purpose? What is the author's main message in the text? *What is the purpose of your argument? What claim are you making?*
- **Perspective of Audience**: Who is the audience? What is the perspective of the author? What other perspectives should be considered when developing the argument? *What is your perspective? What other perspectives should you consider?*
- *Techniques:* What specific techniques does the writer use to develop his/her claim (e.g., language, positive and negative word connotations, personification, simile, metaphor, etc.) *What techniques can you use to develop your claim? What tone will you use? How will you use imagery or other visuals to convey your message? How can you use similes or metaphors to compare an idea or issue to something familiar to your audience? How can you exaggerate your point using hyperbole?*
- **Structure/Organization**: How does the writer organize ideas (e.g., problem/solution, cause/effect, point by point, chronologically, sequentially, compare/contrast)? *How are you going to organize your ideas?*
- **Data**: What research, facts, statistics, or expert opinions are used? Are these sufficient? Are statements easy to accept or does the author need to provide more evidence? *How will you use research, facts, statistics, or expert opinions to support your claim or idea? If using a graph, is your data represented accurately? What message does your data suggest?*
- **Emotions/Personal Connections**: How does the writer appeal to the audience's emotions? *How can you use emotional appeals and connections to influence the audience? What stories or examples can you share with the audience?*
- **Credibility and Trustworthiness:** Is the writer credible? Are sources credible? What does the author do to establish trust? *How can you establish your own credibility? How can you show the audience that you are knowledgeable on this topic? Do you explore counterarguments? How can you refute these opposing claims with additional facts or data?*
- **Implications**: What are the short-term and long-term consequences of this argument or message? *What are the positive and/or negative effects of the argument or message?*
- **Evaluation**: How effective is the writer in developing his/her claim? To what extent is the purpose fulfilled? Is there a balance of feelings and emotions, credibility, and data? *How have*

you considered all elements of the Argumentative Writing Wheel? Have you incorporated multiple perspectives and opposing ideas into your writing? What techniques did you use to build your argument and appeal to your audience?

Examples of Complex Questions for Writing

- **Techniques + Emotions/Personal Connections:** *What word connotations or imagery does the writer use to evoke emotion in the audience?*
- **Emotions/Connections + Data:** *How can you balance emotional appeals with facts and information?*
- **Data + Credibility and Trustworthiness:** *How can you refute opposing claims with additional facts or data?*

BLANK ARGUMENTATIVE WRITING ANALYSIS WHEEL

Directions: Draw arrows across elements to show connections.

Text: _____

Purpose/Context

- Point of View and Audience
- Data
- Techniques
- Structure and Organization
- Emotions and Personal Connections
- Purpose or Claim
- Credibility and Trustworthiness

Created by Tamra Stambaugh, Ph.D., & Eric Fecht, Ed.D., 2018. Adapted from Mofield & Stambaugh, 2015.

ARGUMENTATIVE WRITING ANALYSIS WHEEL GUIDE

Directions: Draw arrows across elements to show connections.

Text: _____

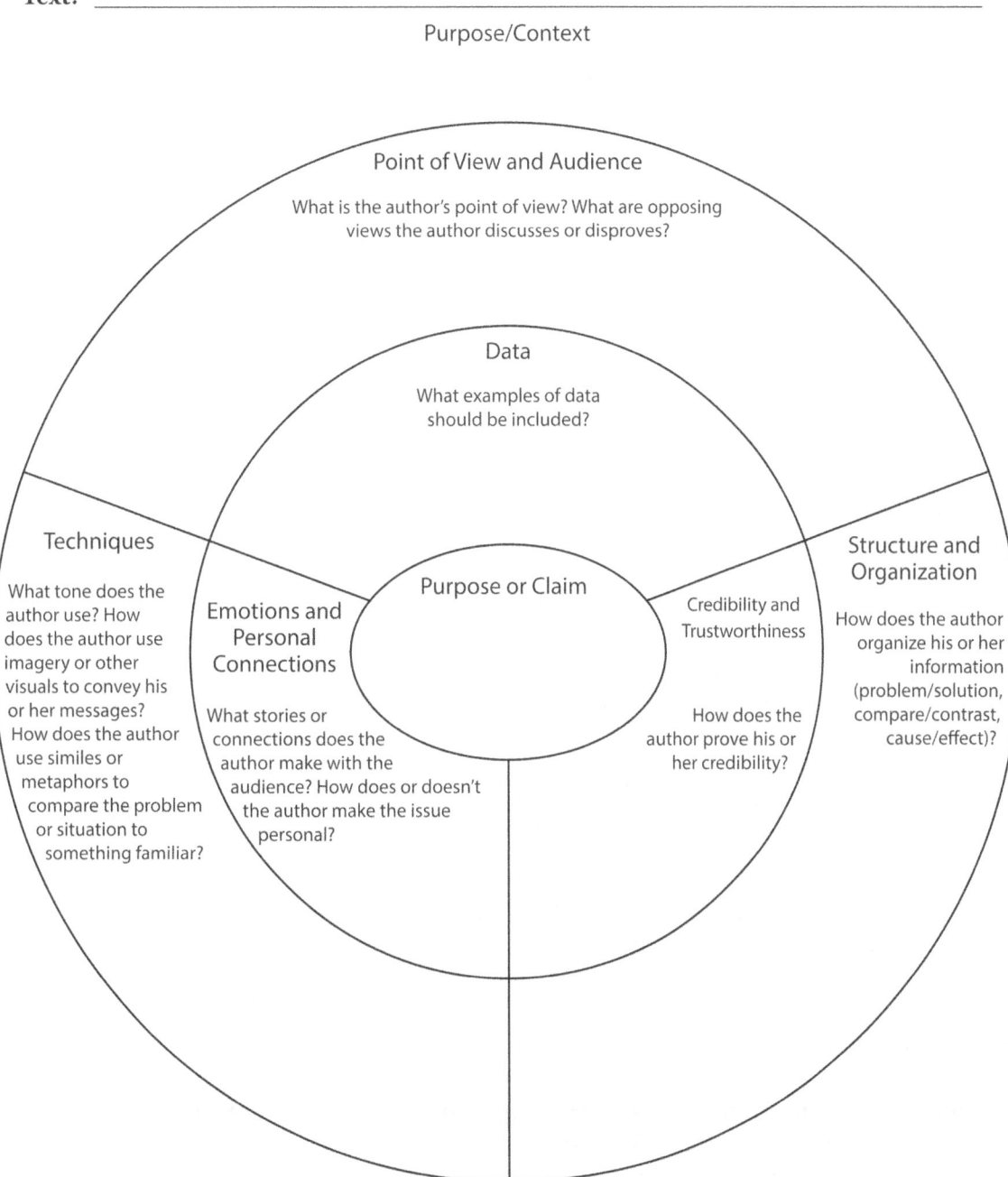

Created by Tamra Stambaugh, Ph.D., & Eric Fecht, Ed.D., 2018. Adapted from Mofield & Stambaugh, 2015.

Appendix A7

Social Studies Connections Wheel

Examples of Simple Questions

- **Historical Key Idea**: What is the main historical event, person, or idea you are studying?
- **Economics**: What is the economic situation? What are the main goods and services? What resources are available? How do we see the concepts of consumption and scarcity?
- **World Context**: What else is happening in the world at this time? What other movements are taking place? How do other world events connect?
- **Politics/Power**: What type of government is in place? What laws are relevant to this idea? Who is in power? What is the role of alliances?
- **Social Structure**: What issues of equity do you notice? What were the needs of families during this time? How does education relate? How is society structured? What hierarchies are in place? What are the social conditions?
- **Culture**: What religious values are relevant? What art, literature, or music relates to this topic? What is the role of nationalism and identity?
- **Geography**: Where do people move? How does the environment affect the people? How does location impact how they live? What is the impact of diffusion?
- **Innovation**: What new tools and technology have emerged? How has communication evolved? How does science relate to this topic?
- **Conflict**: What problems are the people experiencing? What wars are relevant? What internal and political conflicts are happening?
- **Implications**: What are the short-term and long-term implications of the historical key idea? What are the positive and negative implications? How did this event/idea lead to problems, solutions, or new ideas?

Examples of Complex Questions

- **Geography + Innovation**: How does geography influence innovation for transportation, energy, communication, and basic needs?
- **Economics + Politics/Power + Conflict:** How did economic and political factors interact to cause conflict?
- **Historical Key Idea + Geography + Economics:** How does the problem of study relate to the economic and geographic context?
- **Implications + Historical Key Idea + Social Structure:** What were the long-term implications of the event on the economic structure of ___?

Stambaugh, T., & Mofield, E. (2022). *A Teacher's Guide to Curriculum Design for Gifted and Advanced Learners: Advanced Content Models for Differentiating Curriculum.* Routledge.

BLANK SOCIAL STUDIES CONNECTIONS WHEEL

Directions: Draw arrows across elements to show connections.

Text: _____

Context/Era

- Economics
- Innovation
- Politics and Power
- Geography
- Social Structure
- Conflicts
- Historical Key Idea
- World Context
- Culture

Implications
Consider how each of the factors interact to produce problems, solutions, and new ideas.

Created by Emily Mofield, Ed.D., & Tamra Stambaugh, Ph.D., 2015.

SOCIAL STUDIES CONNECTIONS WHEEL GUIDE

Text: _____

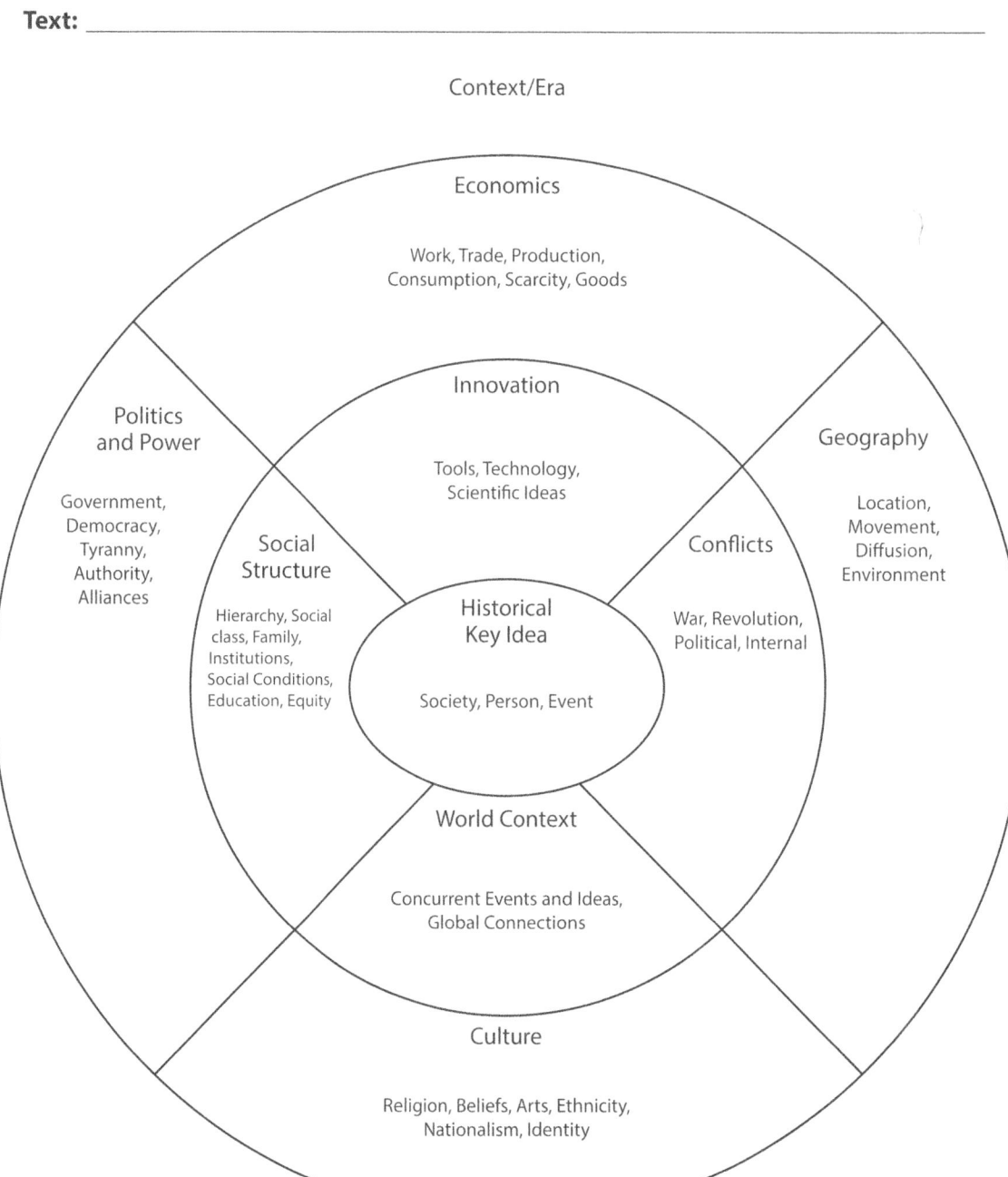

Created by Emily Mofield, Ed.D., & Tamra Stambaugh, Ph.D., 2015.

Appendix A8

Primary Source Analysis Wheel

Simple Questions

- **Purpose (Author's Purpose and Learner's Purpose)**: What is the author's purpose in creating this? What is my goal as I study this source? Note: the learner's purpose will vary depending on the lesson purpose established by the teacher.
- **Point of View:** What is the author's point of view? What assumptions are made? Are biases present? What were others' points of view about this source? What is my point of view? How can this be viewed from an economic perspective? Political perspective? Geographic perspective?
- **Context**: When and where was this written? What else was happening during this time? Globally? Locally? Prior to and after?
- **Impact/Influence**: What is the impact of this document over time? On the current day? On the future?
- **Author/Audience**: Who is the author? Who is the intended audience?
- **Issue**: What is the main issue or problem in the document?
- **Main Idea/Concepts**: What are the main points being made in this source? What concepts or ideas do you see in this source?
- **Credibility**: How reliable is this source? How do you know? Can we trust the source? Does the language used match the time period?
- **Organization/Techniques**: How are the information/images organized? Why? What specific techniques are used? How is the message crafted?
- **Evidence**: What details do I notice? What other evidence do I need? What other corroborating evidence is needed? What inferences can I make from this evidence? What questions do I need to ask?

Example of Complex Questions

- **Issue + Impact + Evidence**: What was the impact of the issue noted in the primary source document? What evidence do you need to answer this question?
- **Organization/Techniques + Main Idea/Concepts:** How does the organization and structure support the main idea of the document?
- **Author/Audience + Issue:** How does the issue affect the audience? How do you know?
- **Point of View + Context:** What assumptions are made if viewed from a local context and how is this different from assumptions made from a global context?

Stambaugh, T., & Mofield, E. (2022). *A Teacher's Guide to Curriculum Design for Gifted and Advanced Learners: Advanced Content Models for Differentiating Curriculum.* Routledge.

PRIMARY SOURCE ANALYSIS WHEEL

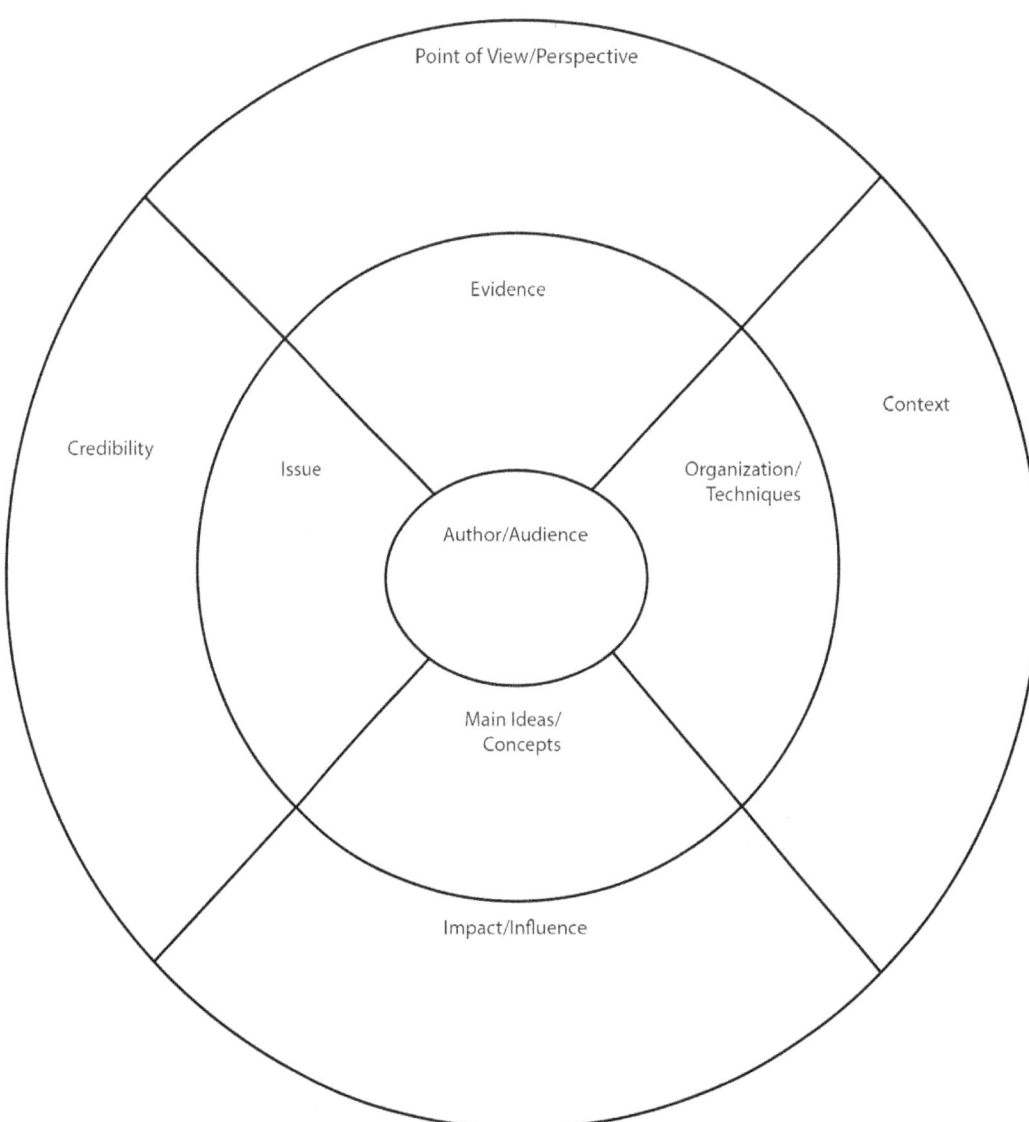

Created by Tamra Stambaugh & Emily Mofield, 2022

PRIMARY SOURCE ANALYSIS WHEEL GUIDE

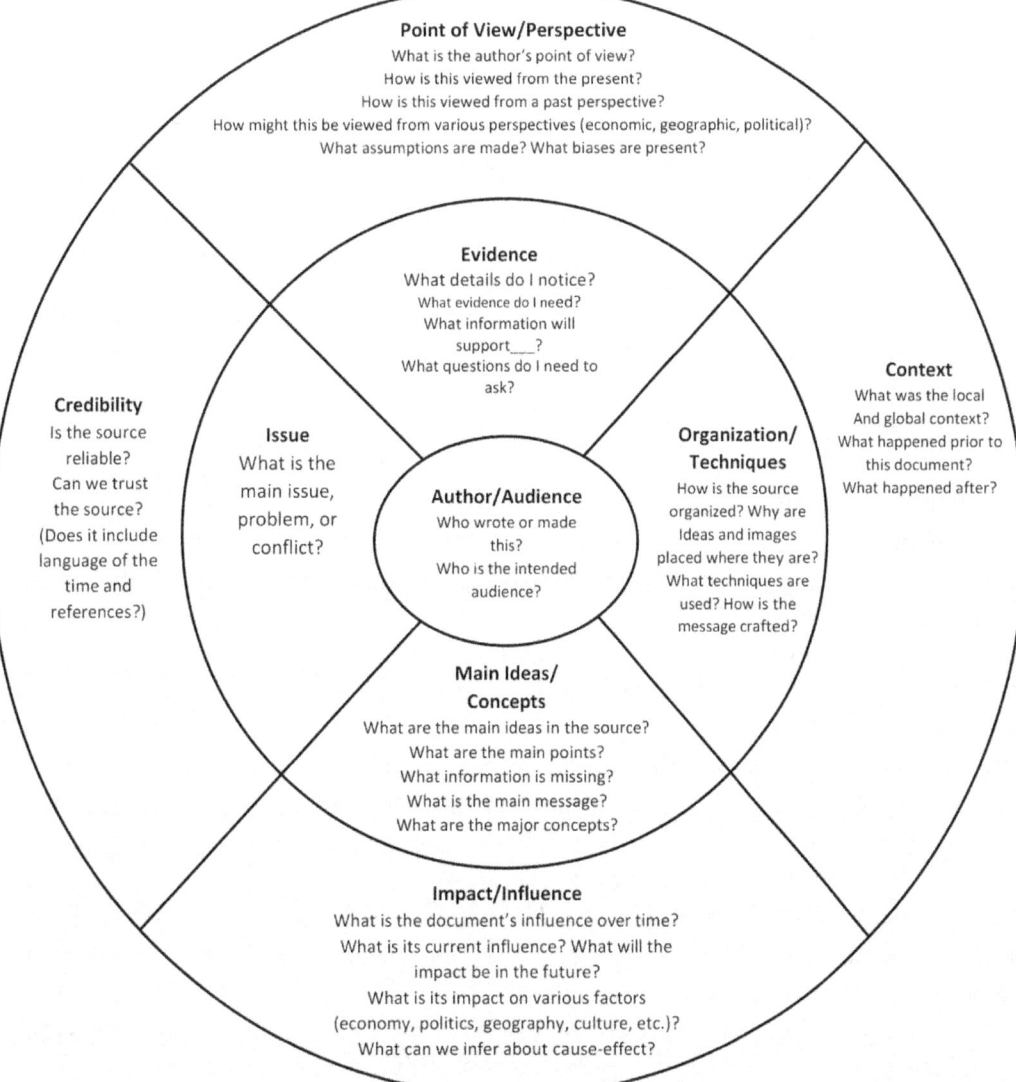

Created by Tamra Stambaugh & Emily Mofield, 2022

Appendix A9

STEM Analysis Wheel

Examples of Simple Questions

- **Idea/Hypothesis Question:** What solution idea should be tested? What is your hypothesis? What question do you have about the problem, issue, or topic? What do you need to know? What do you want to know?
- **Cause and Effect:** What cause-and-effect relationships exist within the problem or hypothesis? What evidence supports the causality? What are multiple causes of the phenomenon? What are the multiple effects of the problem? Of the solution? What contributes to the cause-effect relationships? How does cause-effect allow for prediction? Engineering: How can you design cause-effect?
- **Systems/Energy and Matter:** How does energy or matter flow in and out of the system you are exploring? How does the flow of energy or matter help you understand the issue or topic you are exploring? How is energy transferred within the system you are exploring? What are the input, output, interactions, and boundaries of the system? What elements of a system need to be considered when___? What subsystems influence the larger system? How? How do external systems affect this system?
- **Stability and Change:** What changes have occurred as a result of ___? What causes or prohibits stability in ___? What natural systems create stability or change? How does ___ affect stability/change in ___? What does not change?
- **Patterns:** What patterns do you notice? How can you model or graph this to show trends? How would you classify or categorize this information? What can you predict from these patterns? How does this pattern help us understand relationships between___ and___?
- **Scale and Proportion:** How can you measure or quantify ____? What scale is being used to inform your understanding of the issue? To what extent does the scale influence ____? What is the magnitude of ____? What is the best way to measure____? What is the effect of length of time on ____?
- **Structure and Function**: What are the parts? What are the functions? How does the structure of ____ determine ____? How is a ____ (living or nonliving thing) shaped based on its structure? What substructures determine ____ (properties or functions)? How are the parts related?
- **Scientific Information**: What are the existing scientific principles that relate to the issue? What are the guiding assumptions? What rules, laws, and theories need to be considered? What additional topics in science are connected to the issue or hypothesis being explored? What relevant concepts/topics do you need to study or apply to ____? What other scientific explanations need to be considered?

- **Evidence/Data:** What questions do you have about ____? What data are informing your questions? How do your evidence/data support or refute the findings of others? What data or evidence do you need to collect in order to ____? What inferences can you make? What can you predict from this data?
- **Perspectives/Audience:** What other perspectives need to be considered as you begin to explore your problem/hypothesis? What perspective are you considering now? How might different scientists look at this differently? Who is the intended audience? What process would a ____ (type of scientist) follow to ____? What process do you need to follow? Have you considered or examined perspectives that do not agree with your ideas? What are the pros and cons of various perspectives?
- **Findings/Solutions:** What do you do next with your findings? What inferences can you make about ____? How do you communicate or model your findings or ideas? How would the outcome be different if a different variable or element were isolated or studied? What other solutions have worked? What are the limitations of your findings? Of others' findings? To what extent can these findings be generalized or applied to broader contexts or other populations?
- **Modeling:** How can you model your thinking in a way that shows what will or might happen as a result of ____? How can you best create a model to represent your ideas (diagram, prototype, analogy, illustration)? How might you evaluate, test, or revise your model? What are the limitations of your model?
- **Process/Methods:** What processes or methods are most suitable for solving the problem or testing your hypothesis? Which variables or changes are you isolating for study? Are your methods articulated in a way that allows for replication? Are your methods fair? What are the limitations and flaws to your methods?

Examples of Complex Questions

- **Systems/Energy Matter + Patterns:** What patterns can be found within a system, and how do they influence the flow of energy and matter?
- **Scientific Information + Cause and Effect:** How do scientific theories and relevant concepts influence your understanding of the cause-effect relationship?
- **Structure and Function + Modeling:** How might you create a model to represent the structure, parts, function, and interactions of parts?
- **Scale and Proportion + Findings/Solutions:** How does the scale that is used influence the findings?
- **Patterns + Scientific Information:** How are patterns used to support or inform scientific theories?

Stambaugh, T., & Mofield, E. (2022). *A Teacher's Guide to Curriculum Design for Gifted and Advanced Learners: Advanced Content Models for Differentiating Curriculum.* Routledge.

BLANK STEM ANALYSIS WHEEL

Real-World Issue or Problem: _____

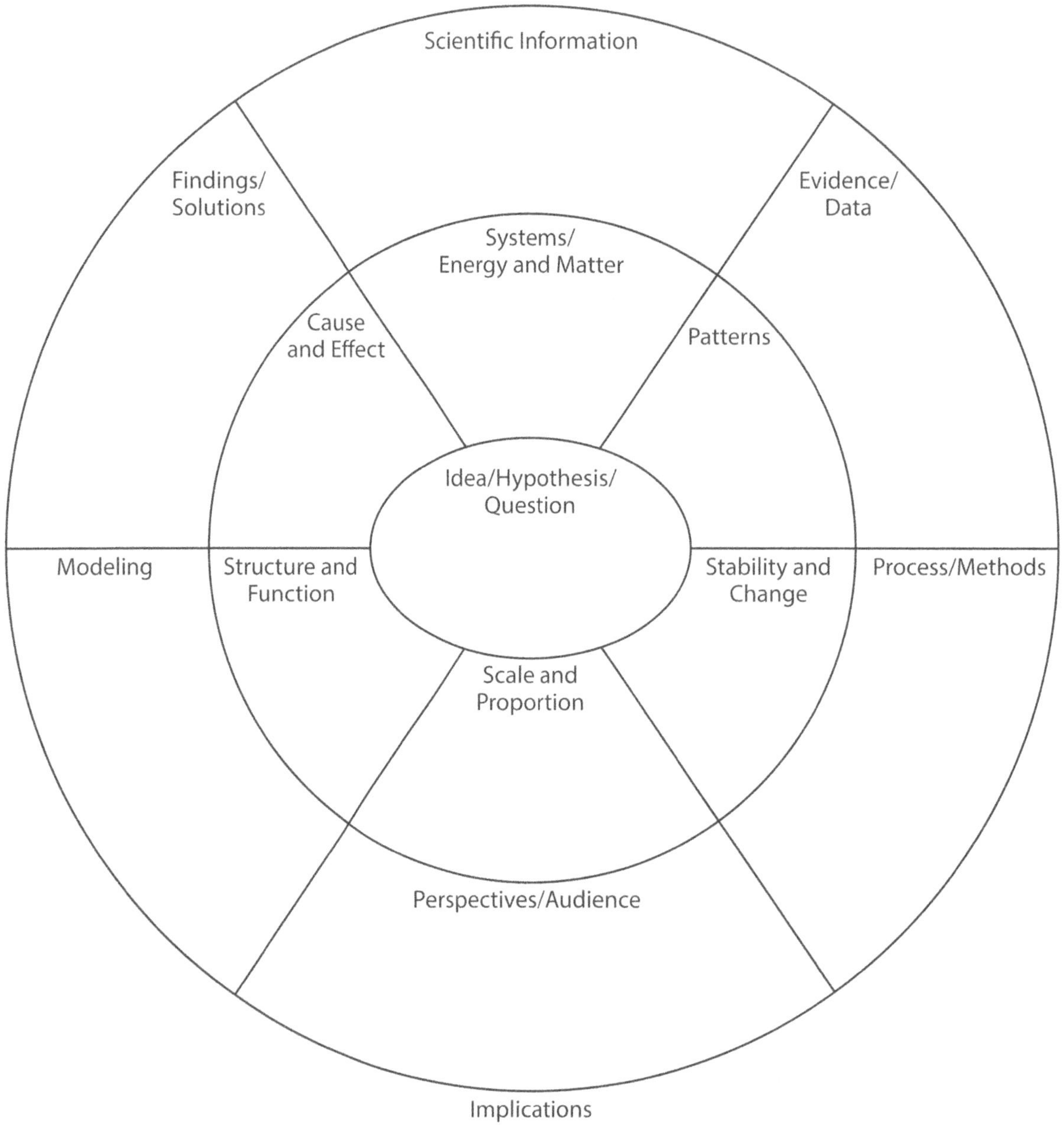

Created by Tamra Stambaugh, Ph.D., & Emily Mofield, Ed.D., 2017.
The middle section of the Science Analysis Wheel is adapted from the Next Generation Science Standards Crosscutting Concepts (National Research Council, 2012).

STEM ANALYSIS WHEEL GUIDE

Real-World Issue or Problem: _____

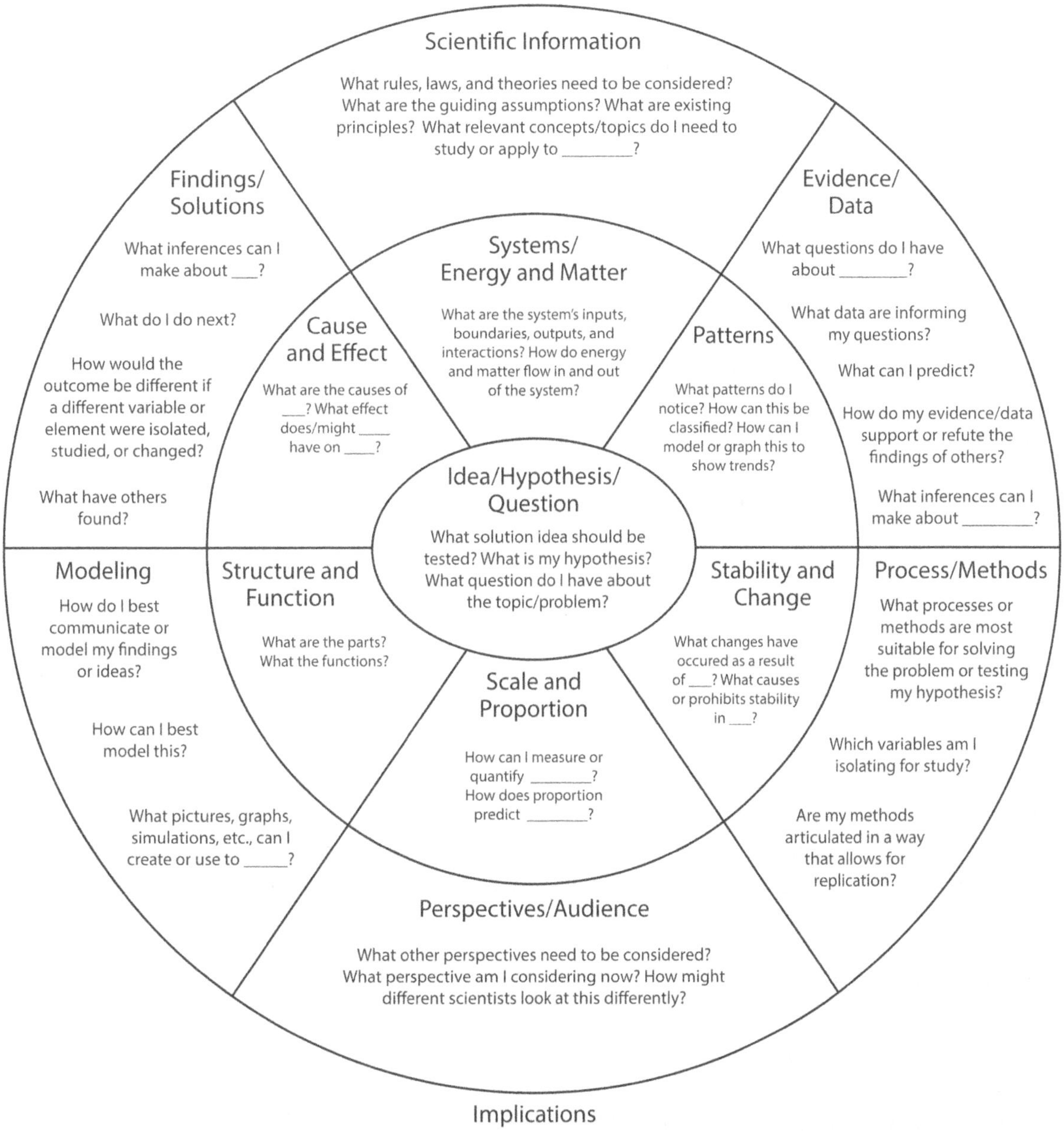

Scientific Information
What rules, laws, and theories need to be considered? What are the guiding assumptions? What are existing principles? What relevant concepts/topics do I need to study or apply to _____?

Findings/Solutions
What inferences can I make about ___?

What do I do next?

How would the outcome be different if a different variable or element were isolated, studied, or changed?

What have others found?

Evidence/Data
What questions do I have about _____?

What data are informing my questions?

What can I predict?

How do my evidence/data support or refute the findings of others?

What inferences can I make about _____?

Cause and Effect
What are the causes of ___? What effect does/might ___ have on ___?

Systems/Energy and Matter
What are the system's inputs, boundaries, outputs, and interactions? How do energy and matter flow in and out of the system?

Patterns
What patterns do I notice? How can this be classified? How can I model or graph this to show trends?

Idea/Hypothesis/Question
What solution idea should be tested? What is my hypothesis? What question do I have about the topic/problem?

Modeling
How do I best communicate or model my findings or ideas?

How can I best model this?

What pictures, graphs, simulations, etc., can I create or use to _____?

Structure and Function
What are the parts? What the functions?

Scale and Proportion
How can I measure or quantify _____?
How does proportion predict _____?

Stability and Change
What changes have occurred as a result of ___? What causes or prohibits stability in ___?

Process/Methods
What processes or methods are most suitable for solving the problem or testing my hypothesis?

Which variables am I isolating for study?

Are my methods articulated in a way that allows for replication?

Perspectives/Audience
What other perspectives need to be considered? What perspective am I considering now? How might different scientists look at this differently?

Implications

Created by Tamra Stambaugh, Ph.D., & Emily Mofield, Ed.D., 2017.
The middle section of the Science Analysis Wheel is adapted from the Next Generation Science Standards Crosscutting Concepts (National Research Council, 2012).

Appendix A10

Visual Analysis Wheel

Examples of Simple Questions

- **Purpose**: What is the purpose of the art?
- **Context**: What year was this art created? What artistic movements may have influenced this work? What type of art is this? What historical events were happening at the time this was made? Is there a specific audience for which the art was created?
- **Main Idea/Message**: What is the main idea of this art? What is the message of the art?
- **Techniques**: What specific techniques does the artist use? (Consider color, shape, brushstroke, patterns, contrast.)
- **Point of View/Assumptions**: What is the artist's point of view toward the topic? What assumptions does the artist make? What is the artist's unstated premise or belief? What does the artist take for granted about the audience?
- **Structure**: How does the artist organize ideas? What is the central part of the painting? Where is your eye drawn first? Why?
- **Images/Symbols**: What are the main images? Do they symbolize a deeper meaning? How?
- **Emotions**: What emotions does this art evoke in you? What emotions does this art reveal/portray?
- **Implications:** What are the short-term and long-term consequences of this art? What are the implications for you after viewing this art?
- **Evaluation:** Do you like this art? Why or why not? Use specific elements from the wheel in your answer. What elements of this art are most important to consider and why?

Examples of Complex Questions

- **Images+ Purpose/Context:** How does the historical context influence the artist's choice of images in his art?
- **Images + Structure:** Why does the artist intentionally place the objects where they are?
- **Artist Background + Purpose/Context:** How is the artist influenced by the historical context of his/her time? How does the artist influence the historical context of his/her time?
- **Emotions + Point of View/Assumptions:** How does the artist's point of view toward the topic influence your emotional reaction to the art?

Stambaugh, T., & Mofield, E. (2022). *A Teacher's Guide to Curriculum Design for Gifted and Advanced Learners: Advanced Content Models for Differentiating Curriculum.* Routledge.

BLANK VISUAL ANALYSIS WHEEL

Directions: Draw arrows across elements to show connections.

Art Piece: _____

Purpose/Context

Point of View

Images

Techniques

Emotions

Main Idea

Artist Background

Structure/Organization

Implications

Evaluation

Created by Tamra Stambaugh, Ph.D., & Emily Mofield, Ed.D., 2015.

VISUAL ANALYSIS WHEEL GUIDE

Directions: Draw arrows across elements to show connections.

Art Piece: _____

Purpose/Context

Point of View

What is the artist's point of view toward the topic?
What assumptions are made?

Images

What are the prominent images?
What might they represent?

Techniques

Visual Effects, Color, Lines, Shape, Movement, Contrast, Placement, Brushstroke, Pattern

Emotions

What emotions are portrayed? What emotions are evoked?

Main Idea

What is the main idea, theme, or message?

Artist Background

What is the artist's background?

Structure/Organization

Where are your eyes drawn first? How does the placement of images influence meaning? How is the art structured?

Implications

What are the short-term and long-term implications of this art?

Evaluation

Do you like this art? Why?

Created by Tamra Stambaugh, Ph.D., & Emily Mofield, Ed.D., 2015.

Appendix B Models for Depth

Appendix B1

Choice-Reasoning Chart – Humanities

CHOICE-REASONING CHART- HUMANITIES

Should or Debatable Question			
Stakeholder, Event or Character's Purpose or Goal			
Choice 1		Choice 2	
Assumption		Assumption	
Evidence/Inference		Evidence/Inference	
Positive Implications (short and long-term)	Negative Implications (short and long-term)	Positive Implications (short and long-term)	Negative Implications (short and long-term)
What other criteria, questions, or information should be considered to achieve the purpose or goal?			

Source: Adapted from "Reasoning about a situation or event" by Center for Gifted Education (2015), retrieved from http://education.wm.edu/centers/cfge/curriculum/teachingmodels. Copyright 2015 by William & Mary, Center of Gifted Education.

Stambaugh, T., & Mofield, E. (2022). *A Teacher's Guide to Curriculum Design for Gifted and Advanced Learners: Advanced Content Models for Differentiating Curriculum.* Routledge.

Appendix B2

Problem-Reasoning Chart – STEM

PROBLEM-REASONING CHART – STEM

Question	
Hypothesis or Problem	

Sources				
Perspective and Assumptions				
Implications				

New Ideas or Questions I Have:	
Other Criteria, Questions, Information to Consider for Interpretation	

Source: Adapted from "Reasoning about a situation or event" by Center for Gifted Education (2015), retrieved from http://education.wm.edu/centers/cfge/curriculum/teachingmodels. Copyright 2015 by William & Mary, Center of Gifted Education.

Stambaugh, T., & Mofield, E. (2022). *A Teacher's Guide to Curriculum Design for Gifted and Advanced Learners: Advanced Content Models for Differentiating Curriculum.* Routledge.

Appendix C Models for Abstractness

Appendix C1

Concept Organizer

CONCEPT ORGANIZER

Generalizations	Source _____	Source _____	Source _____

Appendix C2
Big Idea Reflection

BIG IDEA REFLECTION

What?	**Concepts:** What concepts/ideas are in the text?	
	Generalizations: What broad statement can you make about one or more of these concepts? Make it generalizable beyond the text.	
	Issue: What is the main issue, problem, or conflict?	
So What?	**Insight:** What insight on life is provided from this text?	
	World/Community/Individual: How does this text relate to you, your community, or your world? What question does the author want you to ask yourself?	
Now What?	**Implications:** How should you respond to the ideas in the text? What action should you take? What are the implications of the text? What can you do with this information?	

Created by Emily Mofield, Ed.D., & Tamra Stambaugh, Ph.D., 2015.

References

Adams, W., Wieman, C., & Schwartz, D. (2008). Teaching expert thinking. Retrieved from www.cwsei.ubc.ca/resources/files/Teaching_Expert_Thinking.pdf

Bransford, J. D., Brown, A. L., & Cocking, R. R. (2000). *How people learn: Brain, mind, experience, and school.* National Academy Press.

Center for Gifted Education (2015). Reasoning about a situation or event. Retrieved from http://education.wm.edu/centers/cfge/curriculum/teachingmodels

Erickson, L. (2008). *Stirring the head, heart, and soul: Redefining curriculum, instruction, and concept-based learning* (3rd ed). Corwin Press.

Gay, G. (2018). *Culturally responsive teaching: Theory, research, and practice.* Teacher's College Press.

Harvey, R. (2011, November 11). Literature as an art form. *Pulp.* Retrieved from http://journalpulp.com/2011/11/04/literature-as-an-art-form

Mofield, E., & Stambaugh, T. (2016a). *I, Me, You, We: Individuality vs. Conformity. ELA lessons for gifted and advanced learners in grades 6–8.* Prufrock Press.

Mofield, E., & Stambaugh, T. (2016b). *Perspectives of power: ELA lessons for gifted and advanced learners in grades 6–8.* Prufrock Press.

National Council for the Social Studies (NCSS). (2013). *The college, career, and civic life (C3) framework for social studies state standards: Guidance for enhancing the rigor of K-12 civics, economics, geography, and history.* Author.

National Association for Gifted Children (NAGC). (2019). *Pre-K to grade 12 gifted programming standards.* Retrieved from http://www.nagc.org/resources-publications/resources/national-standards-gifted-and-talented-education/pre-k-grade-12.

Olszewski-Kubilius, P., Subonik, R. F., & Worrell, F. C. (2018). *Talent development as a framework for gifted education: Implications for applications and best practices in schools.* Prufrock Press.

Paul, R., & Elder, L. (2019). *Critical thinking: Tools for taking charge of your learning and your life* (3rd ed.). Pearson.

Russell, J. (2016). "Learning design and social studies for gifted and advanced students." In Kettler, T. (Ed.) (2016). *Modern curriculum for gifted and advanced academic students.* Prufrock Press.

Stambaugh, T., Fecht, E., & Mofield, E. (2018). *Interactions in ecology and literature. Integrated science and ELA lessons for gifted and advanced learners in grades 2–3.* Prufrock Press.

Stambaugh, T. (2013, February). *Gifted students and the Common Core: Implications for practice.* Keynote for the Vanderbilt Gifted Education Institute, Programs for Talented Youth, Nashville, TN.

Stambaugh, T. (2018). Curriculum and instruction within a talent development framework. In Olszewski-Kubilius, P., Subotnik, R. & Worrell, F. (Ed.) (2018). *alent development as a framework for gifted education.* Prufrock Academic Press.

Subotnik, R., Olszewski-Kubilius, P., Worrell, F. C. (2011). Rethinking giftedness and gifted education: A proposed direction forward based on psychological science. *Psychological Science in the Public Interest, 12,* 3–54.

Taba, H. (1962). *Curriculum development: Theory and practice.* Harcourt, Brace & World.

Texas Association for the Gifted and Talented (1991). Universal themes and generalizations. Adapted from the *Curriculum Guide for the Education of Gifted High School Students*. Retrieved from https://www.ggusd.us/assets/files/departments/gate/teacherresources/universalthemes/universal-themes-and-generalizations.pdf

UCLA History (2021). *The Public History Initiative of UCLA*. National Center for the Schools. Retrieved from https://phi.history.ucla.edu/nchs/standards-grades-k-4/developing-standards-grades-k-4/historical-thinking

University of Oxford. (2018, February 26). *History of Art at Oxford University*. [Video]. YouTube. https://www.youtube.com/watch?v=I-1AESwLNq8

VanTassel-Baska, J. (1986). Effective curriculum and instructional models for talented students. *Gifted Child Quarterly*, 30(4), 164–169. https://doi.org/10.1177/001698628603000404

VanTassel-Baska, J. & Stambaugh, T. (2007). *What works: 20 years of curriculum and instruction*. College of William and Mary Center for Gifted Education.

Winkler, D.L., Andermann, R., Moore, J., & Backer, D. (2016). Curriculum to challenge gifted learners in the social studies. In Kettler, T. (Ed.) (2016). *Modern curriculum for gifted and advanced academic students*. Prufrock Press.

Authors' Biographies

Tamra Stambaugh, PhD, is the Margo Long Endowed Chair in Gifted Education and an associate professor at Whitworth University, Spokane, Washington. Stambaugh's research interests focus on students living in rural settings, students of poverty, and curriculum and instructional interventions that promote gifted student learning and the development of expertise. She is the co-author/editor of several books including *Identifying and Serving Gifted Students from Low Income Households* (NAGC Book of the Year – Scholar Category, with Paula Olszewski-Kubilius), *Comprehensive Curriculum for Gifted Learners* (with Joyce VanTassel-Baska), *Overlooked Gems: A National Perspective on Low-Income Promising Students* (with Joyce VanTassel-Baska), *Leading Change in Gifted Education* (with Bronwyn MacFarlane), the *Jacob's Ladder Reading Comprehension Series (Fiction, Nonfiction, and Affective)* (with Joyce VanTassel-Baska), *Practical Solutions for Under-represented Gifted Students: Effective Curriculum* (with Kim Chandler), *Identifying and Serving Gifted Students in Rural Settings* (Legacy Award Winner – Scholar Category) (with Susannah Wood), and multiple award-winning English Language Arts (ELA) and ELA/science curricula (with Emily Mofield and Eric Fecht). Stambaugh has also written numerous articles and book chapters. She frequently provides keynotes, professional development workshops, and consultation to school districts nationally and internationally and shares her work at refereed research conferences. She serves on the National Association for Gifted Children (NAGC) Board of Directors and is a reviewer and editorial board member for several leading research journals in the field of gifted education.

Stambaugh is also the recipient of multiple awards including: the *Margaret The Lady Thatcher Medallion* for scholarship, service, and character from the College of William and Mary School of Education, the *Doctoral Student Award, Early Leader Award*, and several curriculum awards from the National Association for Gifted Children; the *Jo Patterson Service Award and Curriculum Award* from the Tennessee Association for Gifted Children, the *Higher Education Award* from the Ohio Association for Gifted Children, and the *Distinguished Vanderbilt Faculty Award for Service to Field*, Peabody College, Vanderbilt University. Prior to her appointment at Whitworth, Stambaugh was Director of Grants and Special Projects at the College of William and Mary, Center for Gifted Education where she earned her Ph.D. and an associate research professor and Executive Director of Programs for Talented Youth at Vanderbilt University.

Emily Mofield, EdD, is an assistant professor at Lipscomb University, Nashville, Tennessee, where she teaches gifted education and doctoral research courses. Mofield has over 20 years of experience in gifted education, recently serving as the NAGC Chair for Curriculum Studies. She has co-authored numerous NAGC award-winning advanced language arts curriculum units (with Tamra Stambaugh, Vanderbilt Programs for Talented Youth). She is also the author/co-author of several research publications and book chapters related to achievement motivation, collaborative teaching practices, and curriculum design. She is the co-recipient of the *NAGC Hollingworth Award for Excellence in Research* and the Texas Association for Gifted and Talented 2019 *Legacy Book Award for Teaching Tenacity, Resilience, and a Drive for Excellence* (with Megan Parker Peters). Recently she has co-authored *Collaboration, Coaching, and Coteaching in Gifted Education* (2021 NAGC Book of the Year – Practitioner Category), and also *Coaching in Gifted Education: Building Capacity and Catalyzing Change* (both with Vicki Phelps). Mofield regularly provides consultation and leads professional learning addressing collaborative teaching and use of differentiation strategies for advanced learners for school districts, conferences, and special groups.

Mofield is also the recipient of the *Jo Patterson Service Award* and *Curriculum Award* from the Tennessee Association for the Gifted, and the 2021 *Dean's Award* from the College of Education of Lipscomb University for significant contributions to the field of education.

For Product Safety Concerns and Information please contact our EU representative GPSR@taylorandfrancis.com
Taylor & Francis Verlag GmbH, Kaufingerstraße 24, 80331 München, Germany

www.ingramcontent.com/pod-product-compliance
Lightning Source LLC
Chambersburg PA
CBHW080939300426
44115CB00017B/2878